KT-450-470

PHILIP ALLAN
LITERATURE GUIDE
FOR GCSE

AQA ANTHOLOGY: MOON ON THE TIDES
CHARACTER AND VOICE, AND PLACE

Margaret Newman

Series editor: Jeanette Weatherall

PHILIP ALLAN
UPDATES

Philip Allan Updates, an imprint of Hodder Education, an Hachette UK company, Market Place, Deddington, Oxfordshire OX15 0SE

Orders

Bookpoint Ltd, 130 Milton Park, Abingdon, Oxfordshire OX14 4SB
tel: 01235 827827
fax: 01235 400401
e-mail: education@bookpoint.co.uk
Lines are open 9.00 a.m.–5.00 p.m., Monday to Saturday, with a 24-hour message answering service. You can also order through the Philip Allan Updates website: www.philipallan.co.uk

© Margaret Newman 2011
ISBN 978-1-4441-2146-9
First printed 2011

Impression number 5 4 3
Year 2016 2015 2014 2013

Cover photo reproduced by permission of MAXFX/Fotolia

Printed in Spain

Hachette UK's policy is to use papers that are natural, renewable and recyclable products and made from wood grown in sustainable forests. The logging and manufacturing processes are expected to conform to the environmental regulations of the country of origin.

P01791

Contents

Introduction

This guide is intended for you to use throughout your GCSE English literature course. It will help you when you are studying the poems for the first time and also during your revision. It explores in detail all the poems in the 'Character and voice' and 'Place' clusters in your anthology. There is also advice on how to compare the poems and how to make sure you demonstrate the correct skills when writing about them. Enjoy referring to the guide, and good luck in your exam.

Features of this guide

The following features have been used throughout this guide:

> ● **Which aspects of the poem should I compare?**

Introductory questions are provided at the beginning of some sections. Check you have understood each of these before you move on.

> **Grade *booster***

Pay particular attention to the **Grade booster** boxes. Students with a firm grasp of these ideas are likely to be aiming for the top grades.

> **Pause for thought**

Develop your thinking skills by answering questions in the **Pause for thought** boxes. You might gain extra insight into the poem.

>
> **Key quotation**
> every pixel of that man's skin
> is shot through with indelible ink

Highlighted for you are **key quotations** that you may wish to use as evidence in your examination answers.

> **Grade *focus***

To help you give a higher-level response, **Grade focus** boxes compare responses at different levels.

> **Review your learning**

Test your knowledge after you have read some of the sections in the **Review your learning** boxes. Answers are available to download at www.philipallan.co.uk/literatureguidesonline.

 Don't forget to go online for further self-tests on the poems: **www.philipallan.co.uk/literatureguidesonline**. You can also find more exam responses at grade C and A* and a glossary of literary terms.

How to approach poetry

A poet's work is to name the unnameable, to point at frauds, to take sides, start arguments, shape the world, and stop it from going to sleep.

Salman Rushdie

Of our conflicts with others we make rhetoric; of our conflicts with ourselves we make poetry.

William Butler Yeats

Poetry was never written to be studied in an examination. It has always been written — and will continue to be written — to explore ideas and emotions and inspire us. The examiners who chose the poems for the anthology themes have tried to offer you a wide selection of experiences, introducing you to famous poets from our literary heritage, as well as an interesting variety of contemporary poets.

When you meet a new poem for the first time, do not try to solve it as though it is a puzzle testing your intelligence. Instead, read it through a few times, perhaps read it aloud, and get a feel for what it is trying to say. It does not matter if there are words you do not understand. Plato, the classical Greek philosopher, is reported to have said: 'Poets utter great and wise things which they do not themselves understand.'

What does matter in the exam is that you are able to give a personal response to the poems you write about, analysing the poets' ideas and techniques to present your opinions. The poets were not afraid to express their ideas, so do not be afraid to express yours.

How to use this guide

You may find it useful to read sections of this guide when you need them, rather than reading it from start to finish. For example, you could read the notes and information on individual poems in your chosen theme shortly after you have read the poem for the first time. The sections *Comparing poems* and *Tackling the assessments* will be especially useful in the weeks leading up to the exam.

The information and ideas for each poem are separated into four sections.

Context

This section gives background information about the poet. Although you will not be examined on this, it is often helpful and interesting to know more about the poet and, in the case of the literary heritage poets, the times in which they lived.

What happens?

This section tries to sum up the content of the poem. If there are words you have not met before, you may find an explanation of their meaning in the glossary. When you are responding to a poem, remember that there are not many marks for knowing what it is about. Instead you need to show you understand how a poet shapes a reader's response.

Structure, language, imagery

These sections help you to explore the poem in more detail, so you can recognise the way poets use their skills. Look back at the poem and see whether you agree with the suggestions and whether you can find more examples of the techniques highlighted in bold. There is a *Glossary of literary terms* online to which you can refer. Go to www.philipallan.co.uk/literatureguidesonline and access the material for this guide.

Points to consider

The ideas and questions in this section could really develop your appreciation of the poem. There are usually no right or wrong answers to the questions, but considering the ideas in more detail could gain you extra marks for personal interpretation regarding poets' opinions and purposes.

Comparing poems

The essential skill the examiners expect of you is the ability to compare poems. Remember that comparison involves looking for differences as well as similarities. This section gives you information about the exam, advises you on time management and helps you to plan your response to make sure you compare throughout.

Tackling the exam

This section tells you what to do when the exam starts and why it is important to use your time wisely. There is advice on choosing the question, writing a quick plan, how to start your response, using PEE to achieve high marks, examples of A* responses, and practice questions for foundation and higher tiers. (Go online to read grade-C responses.)

When writing about the poems, use this guide as a springboard to develop your own ideas. Remember: the examiners are not looking for set responses. You should not read this guide in order to memorise chunks of it, ready to regurgitate in the exam. Identical answers are dull. The examiners hope to reward you for perceptive thought, individual appreciation and varying interpretations. They want to sense you have explored the poems, engaged with the ideas and enjoyed this part of your literature course.

Timelines

Although you will not be asked about a poet's life in the exam, an understanding of what it was like to be living when the poem was written should give you further insight into the poet's purpose, language and feelings.

Character and voice

Literary heritage poets

Poet	Poem
Percy Bysshe Shelley, 1792–1822	Ozymandias, 1818
Robert Browning, 1812–89	My last Duchess, 1842
Thomas Hardy, 1840–1928	The ruined maid, 1866
Stevie Smith, 1902–71	The river god (date unknown)
John Betjeman, 1906–84	On a portrait of a deaf man, 1940
Dylan Thomas, 1914–53	The hunchback in the park, 1946
U. A. Fanthorpe, 1929–2009	Casehistory: Alison, 1978

Contemporary poets

Poet	Poem
Dorothy Molloy, 1942–2004	Les grands seigneurs
John Agard, 1949–	Checking out me history
Carol Ann Duffy, 1955–	Medusa
Jackie Kay, 1961–	Brendon Gallacher
Simon Armitage, 1963–	The clown punk Give
Andrew Forster, 1964–	Horse whisperer
Daljit Nagra, 1966	Singh song!

Place

Literary heritage poets

Poet	Poem
William Blake, 1757–1827	London, 1792
William Wordsworth, 1770–1850	Extract from The Prelude, 1805
Emily Jane Brontë 1818–48	Spellbound, 1837
W. B. Yeats 1865–1939	The wild swans at Coole, 1919
D. H. Lawrence, 1885–1930	Storm in the Black Forest, 1929
Norman MacCaig, 1910–96	Below the Green Corrie (date unknown)
Ted Hughes, 1930–98	Wind, 1957

Contemporary poets

Poet	Poem
Gillian Clarke, 1937–	Cold Knap Lake Neighbours
Margaret Atwood, 1939–	The moment
Seamus Heaney, 1939–	The blackbird of Glanmore
Grace Nichols, 1950–	Price we pay for the sun
Kathleen Jamie, 1962–	Crossing the loch
Jean Sprackland, 1962–	Hard water
Simon Armitage, 1963–	A vision

PHILIP ALLAN LITERATURE GUIDE FOR GCSE

Poem by poem

- What is the context of the poem?
- What happens in the poem?
- How is the poem structured?
- How does the poet use language?
- What imagery does the poet use?

Character and voice

Contemporary poems

'The clown punk' by Simon Armitage

Context

Simon Armitage was born in Huddersfield, Yorkshire in 1963 and has lived in this area for most of his life. He draws on the people and places of his own experiences in many of his poems. His use of Northern dialect colours his poetry and the contemporary vocabulary is particularly attractive to young people.

'The clown punk' is a poem from *Tyrannosaurus Rex versus The Corduroy Kid*, his collection of poems published in 2006. In a recent radio interview, Simon Armitage explains how he regularly used to see 'the clown punk' when he was driving around town. He explains how this character once pushed his face up against his windscreen when he was waiting at traffic lights. The occasion when he says he was 'eyeball to eyeball' with this local man was sufficiently memorable to later be the subject of a poem.

Watch Simon Armitage read the poem on YouTube. He humorously comments: 'That's what happened to punk rock from Huddersfield — it became sort of formal poetry!'

Glossary

shonky (l. 1) (*dialect*) poor, run-down, seedy, disreputable

pixel (l. 5) the tiny dots that make up the images on computer displays

indelible (l. 6) impossible to remove, erase, or wash away; permanent

punk (title and l. 10) a member of a rebellious 1970s' youth movement, characterised by harsh lyrics attacking conventional society and popular culture, and often expressing alienation and anger; punk fashion included tattoos, piercings and metal-studded, spiked accessories

slathers (l. 12) (*informal*) spreads thickly

mush (l. 12) (*dialect*) face

What happens?

The poet describes a local character he used to see regularly when driving home. On one occasion, the man he names 'the clown punk', because of his eccentric appearance, presses his face up against the windscreen. Imagine, says Armitage, what this man will look like in thirty years' time, when his tattoos will no longer look fierce and rebellious, but shrunken and distorted on the man's ageing body. The 'clown punk' has foolishly tied himself to his youth.

Structure

The poem is in **sonnet form** with three quatrains and a final couplet. On first reading there appears to be no strong rhyme pattern, but further inspection reveals an interesting shape to the **rhymes**. The first two lines introduce 'the town clown' and have perfect rhymes. At the point where the man is described, the rhyme pattern changes into **half rhymes** and completely falls apart (as the tattooed man would seem to do over the years) in lines nine and ten. As Armitage addresses the readers — 'You kids in the back seat' — the poem picks up a couplet of half rhymes again before the concluding rhyming couplet and its parting message.

Despite three separated quatrains, Armitage uses **enjambement** and **caesura**. The break between 'But' at the end of line 4 and 'don't laugh:' at the start of line 5 has a dramatic effect. The character may look comical, but growing older along with your tattooed skin is no laughing matter and the emphasis on 'But' highlights this.

Language

The sense of security and comfort in the opening words 'Driving home' is instantly challenged with the phrase 'shonky side of town'. The poet has local knowledge of the town where he sets the scene and introduces a local character. 'You'll see the town clown,' he tells us, speaking directly to the reader. This title is ridiculous and carries with it the weight of judgement. The poet's attitude towards the colourful character is initially one of amusement.

Suddenly the tone changes at the beginning of stanza two when the poet again addresses the reader with **imperative verbs**: 'don't laugh', 'think', 'remember'.

As we read the poem we are looking over the poet's shoulder and responding with alarm 'when [the man] slathers his daft mush on the windscreen'. Armitage uses dialect (or slang) words like 'shonky', 'slathers' and 'daft mush' (probably used regularly in his home town of Huddersfield) to give a sense of place and draw the reader in to share his personal experience. Compare the poetic language of lines 9 and 10 with the informal, shocking description that follows. Any face pressed suddenly up against a windscreen would be alarming, but this image is threatening because it is unconventional.

As well as the informal 'shonky' and 'daft' there are other expressive **adjectives**.

- The 'indelible ink' (l. 6) used for tattoos is injected under the upper layers of skin and cannot be removed, often seeming irrelevant and causing embarrassment in later life.
- 'The deflated face and shrunken scalp' are other effects of physical ageing. When we age, the shape of our face changes; the tissue over our cheeks reduces. These changes are rarely welcomed, but their effects on tattooed skin would be noticeably unattractive. Ageing skin loses moisture and elasticity, therefore tattoos would fade and distort.
- The line 'still daubed with the sad tattoos of high punk' is very telling about Armitage's views: 'daubed' suggests the tattoo has been badly done, the way a child would paint hastily and clumsily. The adjective 'sad' ambiguously infers the ridiculous and regrettable state of the ageing punk as well as the poet's disapproval. Or do you think the poet really does feel pity?

Imagery

The 'town clown' is described with the **simile** 'a basket of washing that got up/and walked'. This could be a stereotypical image of a homeless person with all the clothes he/she possesses piled one on top of the other, or, if the clothes are brightly coloured, could suggest the garments of a circus clown.

The use of the **metaphor** 'shot' here is another example of **ambiguity**. Ink is injected under the skin when tattooing, but there is also the sense of an iridescent fabric, as in the material 'shot silk'. Informally, to be 'shot' implies to be ruined and exhausted, so one word conjures up many connotations.

Points to consider

In the 1970s, punks considered the way they looked to be very important, since it needed to express their refusal to conform to the rest of society. Jeans, Doc Martens, red laces, studded jackets, army pants, safety pins, ripped clothes — all these reflected the attitude of their subculture. Is there a present-day equivalent to punk? Would you consider getting a tattoo?

When we are cocooned inside a car there is barrier between ourselves and the world outside. If we do not want to look at the view we can wipe

Grade *booster*

To improve your response, analyse the use of a word or phrase in detail. What does 'his dyed brain' (l. 13) suggest to you? Can you hear the opinion of the poet here? How does it link with the word 'indelible'?

Key quotation

every pixel of that man's skin

is shot through with indelible ink

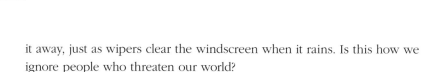

it away, just as wipers clear the windscreen when it rains. Is this how we ignore people who threaten our world?

'Checking out me history' by John Agard

Context

John Agard was born on 21 June 1949 in Guyana (a British colony at the time), on the coast of north-east South America. Guyana gained independence from England in 1966, the year before Agard moved to London. He is a poet, playwright and children's author who often writes about issues of identity and racial conflict. Well known for his eccentric and lively poetry readings, his poems benefit greatly from being performed by their author. He lives and works in Sussex.

> ### Glossary
>
> *1066 and All That: A Memorable History of England* is a satirical account of British history from 55 BC to 1918. It relates historical events as being 'A good thing' or 'A bad thing' and ridicules the way history is taught, in order that Britain appears to be the 'top nation'.

What happens?

In a witty way, Agard protests that British heroes whose names are immortalised in British culture and history books are all white men and women. He names nursery rhyme and folk characters that very young children learn to recognise, but there is little mention of black heroes: their courage, their skills and their persistence. As a black British man, Agard argues that it is essential to know your own identity, to understand your own personality and individuality. He insists that knowledge of your own cultural and racial background will give you this reassurance and confidence. In today's multiracial society he wants to learn about the legendary Africans and West Indians who are part of his Caribbean heritage, not just celebrated white English and European men and women chosen to be taught in history lessons and textbooks.

Pause for thought

Is Agard suggesting that those who choose which historical figures to pass to the young as role models may have a clear political agenda? What might this be?

Structure

The poem is written in free verse with three separated italicised stanzas, each of which describes the impressive skills, personality and achievements of a renowned West Indian who fought to benefit others. Lines 4 and 5 are also set separately from the other stanzas. These important lines shout out the reason for the poet's resentment. Placed between two 'Dem tell me' stanzas, these two lines express Agard's indignation, at the beginning of the poem.

Compare the first and last stanzas. Why are lines 2 and 3 rearranged into the one line 51? Is there a sense of impatience that what he's been taught in the past is no longer important? The last two lines stress his new intentions: he's 'now checking out me own history/...carving out me identity'.

Frequent **rhymes** run irregularly through the stanzas.

- The 'me', 'history', 'identity' pattern emphasises the voice of protest at the start.
- Lines 10–21 rely on half-rhymes — 'vision', 'Napoleon', 'battalion', 'beacon', 'Revolution' to chant and proclaim the accomplishments of the ex-slave who fought to create the first 'black Republic'.
- When Agard performs his poetry he stresses his recurrent rhymes in a forceful, persuasive way. Imagine how he would emphasise the '-oon' rhymes at the end of lines 22–25 to demonstrate his incredulity and the 'go-no-snow' pattern of lines 43–45 to show his admiration.

> **Key quotation**
>
> Bandage up me eye with me own history
>
> Blind me to me own identity

Language

Agard writes in the rhythms and **dialect** of Caribbean Creole. His pride in and affinity with his Guyanese background are probably the reason why he prefers to use this dialect when considering the subject matter of race and ethnicity.

'Toussaint/a slave/with vision/lick back/Napoleon' uses the **slang** verb 'to lick' to give the impression that defeating the conquering troops of Napoleon was quite an easy feat for Toussaint L'Ouverture and his army — that the French were well and truly 'thrashed'.

Agard believes he has been denied knowledge relevant to his own culture by those people in authority who have the power to choose what information he should be given. In order to get his point across strongly, he uses **repetition** for the three words 'Dem tell me'. 'Wha dem want to tell me' is another accusation repeated for effect. The words 'Dem never tell me bout' precede each description of the courageous heroes who should be celebrated alongside those in the English history curriculum.

Words starting with the **plosive letter** 'b' begin lines 4 and 5 — 'Bandage...', 'Bind...', forcing across the poet's resentment.

Imagery

Examine the way that **metaphors** are used to describe the West Indian heroes and heroines.

- Toussaint is 'de thorn/to de French'. In the same way that a thorn in the flesh is painful and difficult to remove, so L'Ouverture and his

army of committed ex-slaves fought hard and continuously to gain their country's independence from the French army who sought to colonise the country that came to be called Haiti.

- He is also named as 'de beacon/of de Haitian Revolution'. A beacon is a guiding light that shines brightly in the darkness. Agard considers Toussaint to be a symbol of inspiration, hope and encouragement: a shining example of courage and fortitude to those he led.
- 'Nanny de maroon' is a magical, mystical figure — 'a see-far' and 'fire-woman', who is described as 'hopeful stream/to freedom river'. Just as a stream rushes down to join the river, so Nanny had great faith and optimism that she could rescue slaves and give them lifelong freedom, 50 years before slavery was abolished.
- Mary Seacole's 'healing star/among the wounded' suggests a shining example of light and hope to injured soldiers, far from home. Where there is no hope of recovery, she becomes 'a yellow sunrise/to the dying'. In her autobiography, Mary Seacole calls herself 'The Yellow Doctress' when she establishes a hotel in Panama and successfully treats victims of cholera.

The metaphorical language used in 'Bandage up me eye with me own history' and 'Blind me to me own identity' implies a definite decision to disallow any knowledge and leave a person 'in the dark'.

'I carving out me identity', Agard exclaims in the last line. He's now actively deciding to read, question and discover who his ancestors were and how they shaped his future. He's no longer accepting information in a passive, unresisting way. Of course, having written this poem, it is very clear that Agard has already checked out his 'own history'.

Points to consider

Had you heard of the historical characters and events named in the poem? Which ones had you never heard of? Do you agree with John Agard's view that a person needs to understand his/her own cultural and racial roots in order to appreciate his/her own identity?

- How is history taught in schools nowadays? Are students given choices when studying history? Internet access gives us opportunities for research that were not possible when textbooks were the only source of information. Do you think young people are interested in 'checking out their history'? Websites for exploring a family tree are certainly popular.
- Agard is making a serious point in this poem, yet he does so by using humour and light-heartedness. Is this an effective way to protest about something that you think is unjust?

'Horse whisperer' by Andrew Forster

Context

Andrew Forster was born in 1964 and grew up in Rotherham in South Yorkshire. He lived in Scotland for 20 years before moving to Cumbria in 2008, where he is Literature Officer for the Wordsworth Trust. 'Horse whisperer 'is from his collection of poems called *Fear of Thunder*, published in 2007. His second collection, *Territory*, was published in May 2010.

'Horse whisperer' is the name given to a person who is able to control the behaviour of a horse. Between the eighteenth and early twentieth centuries, farmers and landowners would pay men, often gypsies, to help to break in their horses and seemingly gain their trust. These men had gentle skills and good horse-sense, combined with knowledge of folklore, ritual and the qualities and effects of herbs and medicinal plants.

Horses were essential to the farmers, who relied on them for ploughing and seed-sowing. Eventually, however, tractors and other machinery replaced the horses. The 'whisperers', whose livelihood depended on these hard-working creatures, were often driven away from their villages and accused of witchcraft, since mystery and secrecy seemed to be essential parts of their craft.

Glossary

rosemary (l. 7) a fragrant herb used in cooking and perfumery

cinnamon (l. 7) dried aromatic bark, used as a spice

wishbone (l. 13) the forked bone attached to the breastbone of most birds

tainted (l. 14) affected by decay

legacy (l. 19) something passed down by ancestors

scorned (l. 23) treated with contempt

hex (l. 26) an evil spell; a curse to bring bad luck

stallion (l. 27) a fully grown male horse

stampede (l. 28) a sudden frenzied rush of panic-stricken animals; the sudden headlong rush or flight of a crowd of people

Shire, Clydesdale, Suffolk (l. 31) breeds of powerful draught (or dray) horses

searing (l. 32) red-hot; fiery

Craig McAteer/Fotolia

Draught horses ploughing

What happens?

The voice or persona of this poem is a horse whisperer. He describes how the farmers would call for him when their horses seemed uneasy and refused to allow themselves to be attached to the plough. He also explains how he was able to calm horses terrified by fire in order to lead them to safety. The skills he used were kept secret in order to ensure that further generations of horse whisperers would always have paid work.

Unfortunately, when farmers acquired tractors, he was no longer required. His skills and practices were denounced and demonised. He had to flee abroad, but not before he took his revenge on the farmers by smearing above the stable doors a substance obnoxious to horses. In the last stanza the whisperer laments his lost relationship with the proud creatures for which, irrespective of his practices, he had a deep admiration and affection.

Structure

The poem is written in five stanzas of **free verse**, the number of lines decreasing with each subsequent stanza. When 'the tractor came over the fields' the stanzas shrink along with the whisperer's fortunes.

The first four words of line 31 are short and surprisingly honest, like a simple heartfelt confession. The last stanza is itself poignantly short: the redundant whisperer realises that his success with horses was due to a shared respect. Andrew Forster says, 'Behind everything in the poem was the bond between the whisperer and the horses, and that suggested the ending. I think it's so powerful because it's so baldly stated in comparison to the rest, and seems to come out of nowhere, though the seeds have been planted.'

To put across the conversational feel of the narrative, **enjambement** is often used. The slight pause before the next line is particularly effective at the end of the first stanza, where the separated line 'to my hands' suggests secret healing qualities.

Look at lines 21/22 and 27/28. Here again the overlapping of the narrative places emphasis on the words 'no longer' and 'no more' — the horse whisperer's days are numbered.

> ### Key quotation
>
> I was the life-blood
> no longer.

Language

'They shouted for me' the first two stanzas begin. The **repetition** reinforces the urgency with which the horses' owners called in the horse whisperer. The verb 'shouted' also provides a contrast to the quiet assured actions of the whisperer when he arrives.

Repetition is again used to full effect in the final lines: '… and the pride,/most of all the pride'. The 'stately' horses, despite having to do strenuous and punishing physical work, still seem honourable and dignified.

The poet must have a fascination with horses: the physical descriptions create strong **visual pictures** with their 'shimmering muscles' (l. 4), 'stately heads' (l. 12), 'searing breath, glistening veins, steady tread' (ll. 32, 33). Reading this poem, a person with little experience of horses would still be able to admire their grandeur.

The phrase 'tender giants' is an oxymoron, since the two words would seem to contradict each other, yet together they reinforce the calming effect of the scented herbs and spices. The 'charm' with which the horses are tranquillised changes to 'a foul hex' on line 26. Both words have the connotation of a magical spell, but whereas 'charm' is pleasing, a 'hex' is a curse.

Look at the use of **alliteration** in line 15. Do you think the repeated sustained 'f' sounds add to the mysterious effect of a 'frog's wishbone' that has rotten meat fastened to it? Perhaps it makes the whisperer himself seem furtive.

> **Pause for thought**
>
> How do we know that the narrator (whether he was using magic or a shrewd knowledge of horse psychology) enjoyed working with the horses and was proud of the bond he shared with such dignified creatures?

> **Grade booster**
>
> 'Then I joined the stampede,/ With others of my kind,' — can you explain why the word 'stampede' is used instead of 'rush', 'charge' or 'flight'? Demonstrate that you can analyse the poet's choice of a particular word, to lift your marks into a higher grade.

Imagery

There are two **similes** in the poem. The terrified horses are led 'like helpless children, to safety' on line 17, due to the controlling effect of the 'tainted wishbone'. When 'the tractor came over the fields/like a warning' the horse whisperer knows he will soon be surplus to requirements.

No wonder the whisperer feels badly treated and resorts to 'the tools of revenge'. This **metaphor** links the arrival of the machine with the horse whisperer using his own devices to achieve results.

Points to consider

Some people believe that the 'whispering' was an act put on to earn a living and that the magic and mystery were all part of the performance, just like a modern-day magician's allegiance to The Magic Circle. Whatever your opinions about the experience required to calm and train a horse — whether you decide that the whisperers were really magical tricksters, gentle horse-lovers or skilled horse behaviour-therapists — you are responding to the poem that is told in the voice of an imagined horse whisperer. You should examine the ways in which the poet has created this voice and how this has made you think and feel.

'Medusa' by Carol Ann Duffy

Context

Carol Ann Duffy was born in 1955 in Glasgow and read philosophy at Liverpool University. A poet, playwright, reviewer and broadcaster, she presently lives and works in Manchester. She is considered one of Britain's most successful and popular poets and became Poet Laureate in 2009.

'Medusa' is from *The World's Wife*, Duffy's collection of poems published in 1999. The poems present characters from history, religion and mythology from the witty and unusual perspective of the women closely connected to the famous males. The poems are sometimes described as 'subversive' since relationships are turned inside out, the wives making fun of their husbands and questioning the concept of male heroism.

The name 'Medusa' today is a symbol of a vindictive monster, but in Greek mythology Medusa was not always ugly. Once she was a beautiful nymph but Athena punished her by turning her into an ugly Gorgon. She had serpents for hair, a protruding tongue and huge fang-like teeth. To prevent further intimacy with a man, Athena inflicted on her the power to turn into stone anybody who looked at her.

The hero, Perseus, was sent on a quest to gain the head of Medusa. He found her asleep, surrounded by petrified creatures. Fixing his eyes on her reflection in his shield, he cut off Medusa's head with his sickle, thrust the head into a shoulder bag and took flight in his invisible helmet. On the way home he revealed the Gorgon's head to the Titan Atlas, transforming him into a mountain and, where drops of blood fell on the desert sand, pits of venomous serpents were created.

Glossary

Gorgon (l. 32) in Greek mythology, one of the three sisters who had snakes for hair and eyes that, if looked into, would turn the beholder into stone; a woman considered ugly and terrifying

What happens?

In this dramatic monologue, Duffy presents an alternative view of Medusa as a woman who, fearing betrayal by her husband, develops terrible physical characteristics alongside a destructive personality. Her husband has great reason to fear her: any life-form she gazes upon is changed instantly into solid matter. She would rather destroy the man she still loves than allow him to be intimate with another woman. Jealousy has turned a once beautiful bride into a vengeful monster.

The Gorgon Medusa

Structure

Although written in free verse, Duffy uses certain kinds of **rhyme patterns**. There is an example of full rhyme at the ends of lines 14 and 17, where the words 'own' and 'stone' complete the first section of the poem; for a 'perfect man' there is a perfect rhyme. Again, as the poem draws to its poignant close, 'tongue' rhymes with 'young' as she makes a last plea to be remembered as she once was.

Elsewhere, **half rhymes** link ideas within a stanza, as in 'foul tongued' and 'yellow fanged' (ll. 8, 9) and 'Gorgon' changes swiftly to 'dragon' in stanza six. Another form of rhyme used is called **assonance rhyme**:

There are bullet tears in my eyes.

Are you terrified? (ll. 10, 11)

The repeated 'eye' sound here adds menace, emphasising her stony feelings.

The final line, separated for dramatic effect, is **ambiguous**. Is Medusa daring her hero to look her in the eyes and succumb to his fate or is she bemoaning her changed state from young beautiful bride to embittered ugly harridan? There is a poignant sadness here as she acknowledges what she has become.

Language

Repetition effectively shows the mood of the speaker:

- 'foul mouthed now, foul tongued' (l. 8) offers images of a furious woman shouting out offensive obscenities;
- 'Are you terrified?' Medusa asks. 'Be terrified.' The repetition of 'terrified' here, combined with the pause between stanzas, also the imperative verb, is extremely threatening;
- 'and your girls, your girls' gives the impression of a stream of young beautiful women, all competitors for the affections of the older man;
- 'Wasn't I beautiful?/Wasn't I fragrant and young?' captures all the pathos in the repeated questions when the Greek God of a husband returns.

Line 6 combines **alliteration** and **oxymoron** for its effect. The 'bride's breath' is expected to be sweet, yet is followed by the words 'soured, stank' — both corrupting verbs with the contemptuous 's' sound, like the thoughts that 'hissed' on line 5. Again the 'b' appears in 'the grey bags', a plosive letter to suggest disgust that the organs responsible for life and oxygen should be reduced to disease-ridden, shapeless sacks. The repeated 'm' when 'Fire spewed/from the **m**outh of a **m**ountain' echoes the 'foul mouthed' offensiveness in stanza two.

Pause for thought

As the persona stares 'in the mirror' she sees 'Love gone bad'. This mirror is the undoing of the mythical Medusa, when Perseus uses his highly polished shield as a mirror. Could having a 'shield for a heart' suggest feelings are reflected away from the truth?

Grade *booster*

To gain marks, analyse the verbs. Violent onomatopoeic verbs describe the resulting effects of the Gorgon's gaze: 'spattered', shattered', 'spewed'. Also the verb sequence begins with 'glanced', then becomes 'looked' and changes into 'stared', as her victims increase in size alongside the intensity of her escalating rage.

Key quotation

Love gone bad
showed me a Gorgon.

Imagery

The **simile** at the beginning of the monologue describes how 'hairs on my head' have been changed 'to filthy snakes,/as though my thoughts/ hissed and spat on my scalp'. Medusa's jealous thoughts have come alive. No longer can she keep her feelings private — her fury boils and seethes around her head like a nest of vipers.

Stanza two uses **metaphors** to describe the physical decay of the jealous wife. 'Bullet tears in my eyes' is an interesting idea. How often do we use tears to wound, to take aim in order to hurt deliberately? The speaker's mood changes here as she shifts from details of how she is physically poisoning herself to hard, cold threats of the harm she can inflict in her desperation.

When the husband arrives 'with a shield for a heart', is he protecting himself from the hurt of looking at what his once beautiful wife has become? Does his heart belong to another beautiful woman? Is he shielding himself from acknowledging his own guilt? He can surely kill with his harsh words: he has 'a sword for a tongue'.

Ideas to consider

The final line invites the 'perfect man' to 'Look at me now'. She is resigned to her fate and would prefer to turn her husband into stone, rather than be ignored. At what stage of the poem do you think she has built the end into her own mind?

When talking about Medusa's husband in a 2005 interview, Duffy says, 'He kills her by betraying her and not loving her.' A once loving relationship has been destroyed. Do you feel sympathy for either character?

The poet is examining the relationship from a jealous wife's point of view. Do you think a male would have different views from a female, when reading this poem?

'Singh song!' by Daljit Nagra

Context

Daljit Nagra's parents came from the Indian side of the Punjab, his father arriving in England in the late 1950s and his mother in the early 1960s. They settled in the London area, where their younger son, Daljit, was born in 1966. In 1982, the family moved north to Sheffield and bought a corner shop in a predominantly white working-class area. Feeling ashamed of his Punjabi background, Nagra met his friends at the door, embarrassed to allow them into his 'Indian' house. When he left school he worked in the family shop by day and studied for his A-levels in the evenings. The family experienced racist attacks and their shop was regularly burgled. Eventually he gained a place to study English at London University.

After university, Nagra trained to become an English teacher. He began to write poetry in his thirties and in 2007 won the Forward Prize (an annual UK award for contemporary poetry) for his collection *Look, We Have Coming to Dover!* 'Singh song!' is from this collection and you can hear Daljit talking about the background to these poems and introducing the opening lines of 'Singh song!' on YouTube: Daljit Nagra — Look We Have Coming to Dover.

He now lives and teaches in London.

Glossary

pinnie (l. 10) abbreviation for pinafore, an apron with a bib to protect clothing

plantain (l. 14) a banana-like fruit that has to be cooked before eating

effing (l. 23) swearing

donkey jacket (l. 33) a short jacket usually made of a thick navy fabric and worn by workmen

What happens?

'Singh song!' is a humorous dramatic monologue narrated in the voice of a young second-generation British-born Asian (Mr Singh), who has been put in charge of one of his father's shops. He is expected to work from nine o'clock in the morning until nine o'clock at night, but when there are no customers he frequently locks the door and runs upstairs to enjoy time with his new wife. Obviously, his customers are not happy, yet their accusation that he runs 'di worst Indian shop/on di whole Indian road' does not worry him in the slightest. His young 'arranged' bride, fashion-conscious, outspoken and excitingly rebellious, is all he can think about. Late at night they cuddle up together in the empty shop and talk about how much they love each other.

Structure

The first four-lined stanza has the form of an introduction. Mischievous in tone, it **rhymes** 'o'clock' and 'lock' to prepare the reader for the saucy goings-on in the next stanza. When the poet performs this poem he often makes a clicking noise on the word 'lock' to illustrate the excitement of locking out the 'shoppers' and rushing upstairs.

> **Pause for thought**
>
> dis dirty little floor need a little bit of mop
>
> in di worst Indian shop
>
> Do you think Mr Singh is speaking with his own Indian accent when repeating what the customers say, or are they mimicking the way he speaks?

The funniest rhymes are probably the 'chutney' and 'Putney' of the second stanza, ridiculous but ideal for demonstrating the exuberance and sexual passion of new married life. 'Putney' is not only an area of London, but also means 'wife' in Punjabi, giving the meaning even more sexual innuendo.

Lines 45 and 47 also have perfect rhyme. Late at night the young couple can be together in the empty shop and once again life is perfect.

Elsewhere there are **half rhymes** (or 'loose rhymes' as Nagra calls them) ending in -y. The three stanzas beginning 'my bride' use words such as 'Punjabi', 'daddy', 'tummy', 'teddy', 'sari', 'sweeties', some of which sound childish. Do you think this gives the impression that Mr Singh is besotted by his bride and reduced to the sentimentalities of sweet talk?

The poem concludes with four (almost) rhyming couplets that break down the structure to suggest the two young lovers with the night to themselves. Nothing gets in the way of their endearments.

The customers' words are written in **italics**, visually separating them from the rest of the poem. This has the effect, therefore, of alienating the young couple from the uninteresting lives of other people, as well as creating a **refrain**.

The use of a **dash** at the end of stanzas is interesting, giving the impression of enthusiastic confidences and a desire to tell all. The final dash perhaps gives the impression that he's sure this state of happiness will continue: 'Is priceless baby —'

Read the poem aloud to hear the **rhythms**. The poet says he 'wanted to write Singh song! as an Indian music hall song'. There is the sense of a lively story being told, sometimes with anapaestic metre ('0 0 -' or 'unstressed, unstressed, **stressed**'). The lines chanted as a refrain are an example:

> in di **worst**/In dian **shop**

> on di **whole**/In dian **road** —

Again the anapaest metre is ideal for the fourth stanza, where a comic rhythm is required to suggest the sound of high heels tapping, a computer mouse clicking or keyboard typing:

> ven she **nett**/ing two **cat**/on her **Sikh**/lov er **site**

Language and imagery

To dramatise the life of the Sikh shopkeeper, Nagra uses the language patterns that Indians use when they speak English instead of their native Punjabi. He is not trying to stereotype his characters, but to allow his readers to share in the joy of the newly-married man when he uses grammar and language that sounds humorous.

The sense of joy and pride is also apparent in the use of **repetition**: 'vee' in stanza two; 'my bride'; 'from di stool each night'.

The descriptions of 'my wife' are **humorous** because of their unex-pectedness: the young woman upstairs is running an online Sikh dating agency (a modern version of arranging marriages). She seems to have little respect for her husband's parents, and her appearance is very unusual, even comical when her only concession to traditional Indian dress is a 'tartan sari'. But Mr Singh is absolutely delighted with her.

The **alliterative** phrase 'tummy ov a teddy' adds to the childlike joyfulness of the speaker and the repeated hard 'c' in 'di precinct is concrete-cool' contrasts with the warmth of the relationship in the 'brightey moon'. Even the stairs are **personified**, their 'whispering' condoning the couple's secret activity.

> **Key quotation**
>
> vee come down whispering stairs
>
> and sit on my silver stool

Grade *booster*

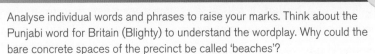

Analyse individual words and phrases to raise your marks. Think about the Punjabi word for Britain (Blighty) to understand the wordplay. Why could the bare concrete spaces of the precinct be called 'beaches'?

Points to consider

Although the poem is humorous and the speaker and his wife seem happy, there are undertones of racial conflict. Whereas there is no excuse for the shop being dirty or the goods out-of-date, the decision to sell limes and plantains for Asian dishes would not be a mistake and the patronising 'dirty little floor' does not suggest honest goodwill. What tone of voice would you use when reading stanzas three and eight out aloud?

There are not many British poets who write about the Asian working classes. Do you think it was a good idea to include this poem in the GCSE Anthology?

'Brendon Gallacher' by Jackie Kay

Context

Jackie Kay was born in 1961 to a Scottish mother and Nigerian father. She and her brother were adopted and brought up in Glasgow, the only black children on their housing estate. From an early age she escaped the real world through her love of reading and writing stories and poetry. She graduated with a degree in English from the University of Stirling in 1983 and published her first book of poetry in 1991. 'Brendon Gallacher' is from her collection of children's poetry entitled *Two's Company*, published in 1992. She was awarded the MBE in 2006 for services to literature and currently teaches Creative Writing at Newcastle University.

Glossary

wee (l. 9) (*Scottish dialect*) small

burn (l. 14) (*Scottish dialect*) a stream

What happens?

'Brendon Gallacher' laments the loss of an imaginary childhood friend. It is easy to imagine this poem as autobiographical, since many of the references link to Kay's family and upbringing. The voice of a six-year-old tells of her seven-year-old imaginary friend, Brendon Gallacher, who, from her point of view, has a far more exciting life than she does. After two years the mother confronts the child with the news that 'there are no Gallachers at 24 Novar' and the treasured imaginary friend has to be killed off. With the loss of her friend, the growing child loses the innocence and freedom of childhood where all things are possible in the imagination.

Structure

Consisting of five stanzas of equal length, the poem has many of the ingredients of a **ballad**: it tells a story, has a song-like rhythm, repeats 'Brendon Gallacher' like a refrain and is sad and romantic. Ballads usually begin by getting straight to the point of the story, just as this poem begins 'He was seven and I was six'. In the same way as many ballads contain the idea of staying loyal and a violent death, so the narrator is constant for two years until Brendon Gallacher meets his sad end, in the dramatic way a child imagines death.

Most of the lines are **end-stopped,** yet on lines 6 and 7 there is an **enjambement** with the lines:

> He would hold my hand and take me by the river
>
> where we'd talk about his family being poor.

The older boy takes control of this sweet and kind relationship. Even at six years old the little girl has the capacity to worry about her friend's family and there's a delightful innocence in the picture of these river walks, spread over two lines to give a sense of contentment and sincerity. The other case of enjambement has a different effect on the reader. The pause after 'Mrs Moir' at the end of line 17 holds the narrative sufficiently for apprehension to creep in before the explanation.

Sing-song rhymes, ending with the letter 'r' sounded, are used to give a musical quality. Words like 'Gallacher', 'burglar', 'worker' have **feminine endings**, where the last syllable is unstressed. Single-syllable line endings such as 'far', 'air' and 'ear' use **half-rhyme** where the final consonant is the same.

Language

The name Brendon Gallacher has a musical rhythm. **Repetition** of the name six times, and always at the end of the line, has the effect of a **refrain** or chorus, like a song. 'Some place nice. Some place far' (l. 9) holds a wistfulness, a desire to get away from mundane dullness. The **pronoun** 'He' is used frequently to emphasise the young girl's attachment to her friend. As a creation of her own mind he truly does belong to her. In the first stanza 'he' and 'I' contrast the different ages, nationalities and family members and the Gallacher family is always much more exciting.

We are reminded that the poet is Scottish by the use of **dialect** with 'wee' (l. 9) and 'burn' (l. 14). The vocabulary used is simple, with the words a child might use.

The gentle **alliteration** in the words 'hold my hand' (l. 6) suggests companionship, while Brendon Gallacher's 'funny, flapping ear' (l. 24) endears the reader to the imagined friend with his detailed idiosyncrasy.

Other physical descriptions of the boy — 'spiky hair' and 'impish grin' use mischievous **adjectives** to convince the reader that he really existed in the little girl's mind. Note that the physical descriptions are given only later. It is his personality that intrigues to make him such a perfect friend.

Key quotation

And he died then, my Brendon Gallacher,

flat out on my bedroom floor

Pause for thought

How does the tone of the poem change in the last stanza? Can you suggest why the lines are shorter?

Grade *booster*

To boost your marks you could analyse why there is such a deep sense of loss and longing in the last line. Explain the effectiveness of the interjected and repeated 'Oh' and the warm familiarity of the first name. Why does the girl mourn somebody who never existed?

The use of **direct speech** gives the poem a sense of immediacy. Whether the mother is inviting the friend 'round to dinner' or remarking that she's been 'talking to Mrs Moir' the words are etched on the little girl's memory. 'No, no I'd say, he's got big holes in his trousers' is a childlike response, but charming in its naivety. The **colloquial** use of 'says' (l. 20) again furthers the sense of a true story.

Points to consider

How does the first reading of the poem contrast with reading it the second time? Do we get the same experience? Can we ever go back to the 'innocence' we had before mum's revelation?

Did you have an imaginary childhood friend? In a 2002 interview in the *Guardian* newspaper, Jackie Kay says that she does not agree with children's imaginations being squashed 'because they're told it's disturbed to have an imaginary friend. The most healthy thing you can have,' she explains, 'is an active and vibrant imagination, because it allows you to carry out all sorts of things without ever actually doing them.' Do you agree with her? The loss of Brendon Gallacher certainly causes a lot of unhappiness.

'Give' by Simon Armitage

Context

'Give' is from Simon Armitage's collection of poetry entitled *The Dead Sea Poems*, published in 1995.

What happens?

'Give' is spoken in the first person. Armitage creates the persona of a homeless person, sheltering in a doorway and desperately begging for money in order to survive. (The speaker could be male or female, but here we presume male.)

Structure

Twelve lines are broken up into five stanzas of two and three lines. This **fragmented form** perhaps suggests the homeless person speaking to different passers-by at different times.

The opening and closing couplets **rhyme** with differing effects. Whereas the first two lines are an introductory couplet, the closing lines (with their repeated 'you') place the emphasis on the public's conscience and sympathy.

'Yours' and 'stars' are examples of **half rhyme** that draw together lines 4 and 5. The third and fourth stanzas are also linked by the use of the similar sounding words 'chains' and 'change'.

The pace of the poem is decided by frequent breaks in the middle of lines. Look at the way a pause is dictated by a comma, dash or full stop, for example: 'I'm on the street, under the stars' (l. 5). This pause is called a **caesura** and, when used regularly, as in this poem, it chops up the ideas to allow the reader to absorb each idea separately and then as a whole.

A regular **iambic tetrameter** beat is used throughout the poem. The lines each have four feet with an iambic stress on the second beat of each foot:

Of **all**/the **pub**/lic **pla**/ces, **dear**

This steady consistent rhythm is like a heart beating and suits a poem that tries to appeal to our emotions with a regular pause after each eight syllables.

> **Pause for thought** ⏸
>
> The iambic stress falls on 'tea' in line 11. Somebody has provided the homeless man with a hot drink, but he does not seem very grateful. Can you think why this is the case? Is it a generous gesture for charities to hand out food and drink to the homeless?

Language and imagery

Living out on the streets all day and night is a long, dreary lifestyle that has a regular pattern to it. Armitage regularly **repeats** words, phrases and the way lines are constructed, which gives a sense of this monotony.

The third stanza uses a **list** format. The homeless man exaggerates what he's prepared to do for donations of money, beginning with 'For coppers' and moving on to 'For silver —' and 'For gold —'. The idea of having to dance and sing like a street performer, in order to be given loose change, is humiliating. To 'swallow swords, eat fire' is dangerous and, along with escaping 'from locks and chains', the kind of dramatic exhibition put on only by experts. Is Armitage suggesting here that members of the public expect something special in return for their generosity, perhaps that they do not recognise that a homeless person has nothing left to 'give'?

The final two lines each use four **single-syllable words**, combined with the **alliterative** words 'big' and 'beg' and the repeated 'you' to put emphasis on the potential giver. It's as though the 'beggar' is saying 'Over to you — the decision is yours — but please help me'.

Because the poem is written in the first person, the pronoun 'I' is often used. The reader's attention is focused on the speaker. The passer-by is addressed at the beginning as 'dear' and later as 'yours'. Only at the end is the pronoun 'you' repeated for dramatic and persuasive effect.

> **Grade booster** ❗
>
> Who do you think the homeless person is addressing? Who is 'you'? Raise your marks by considering the possibilities. Could Armitage be involving the reader here?

Try reading the poem aloud. What tone of voice would you adopt? Are there some words where you allow sarcasm to creep in, or just desperation? How would you say 'dear' on line one and 'That's big of you' towards the end? Imagine yourself in the speaker's situation. Do you think it would be easy to stay polite when people look down on you?

The poem uses colloquial (or conversational) language in a clever way. The idioms used are usually understood as being figurative expressions but, because of this homeless man's situation, they can also be taken literally:

- 'to make a scene' usually means to make a public display or disturbance. Not only is this man on full display but references to 'frankincense and myrrh' also suggest the biblical nativity scene.
- If something is 'on the street' it means 'everybody knows'. This person is literally sitting in the street doorway for all to see.
- To 'hold out' for something as a figurative expression means trying really hard to wait for something or somebody. The persona here is probably trying to hang on to his life in order to survive, while physically holding out his hand or a container hoping to receive money.
- If you are 'on your knees' it means you are no longer managing to cope. In the poem the speaker admits he is absolutely destitute. He is also physically kneeling in the doorway, begging for donations. Note also the link to the Wise Men, who kneel in the Nativity scene.
- 'I beg of you' does not imply just the desperate man's pleading: he is also literally begging.

Points to consider

Why do you think Armitage wrote this poem? A clue to his feelings about homeless people might be on line 10, with the use of the ambiguous word 'change'. Of course, a few loose coins are always welcomed, but do we need to 'change' the way we think about people who have to live on the streets? Is it easier to stereotype the homeless in a negative way than to inform ourselves of the many varied reasons why people end up sleeping 'under the stars'?

'Les grands seigneurs' by Dorothy Molloy

Context

Dorothy Molloy was born in Ireland in 1942. She grew up in County Dublin and studied languages at University College, Dublin, before moving to Spain, where she worked as a painter, historical researcher and journalist. Returning to Ireland in 1979, she continued to paint and write poetry.

'Les grands seigneurs' is from her first collection of poetry called *Hare Soup*, which was published in 2004, ten days after Dorothy's death. Her husband has since assembled more of her poems for two further posthumous collections.

Glossary

Les grands seigneurs (title) French, literally meaning 'the great knights'

buttress (l. 1) a structure, usually brick or stone, built against a wall for support or reinforcement

castellated (l. 1) having turrets and battlements in the style of a castle

bower (l. 2) a shady leafy shelter or recess; a lady's private bedroom

ballast (l. 6) heavy material placed in the hold of a ship to enhance stability

promenade (l. 7) a public area for pedestrians to walk, especially at the seaside

hurdy-gurdy monkey-man (l. 8) probably a street musician who played a small portable barrel organ by turning a handle; this busker would attract an audience by having a pet monkey to collect money and do tricks

courtly love (l. 10) an idealised form of love, celebrated in the literature of the Middle Ages and the Renaissance, in which a knight or courtier devotes himself to a noblewoman who is usually married. She pretends not to be interested to keep her reputation

troubadour (l. 11) a poet who composed romantic songs; a strolling minstrel

damsel (l. 11) a poetic, old-fashioned name for a young, unmarried woman, usually a virgin

call my bluff (l. 15) to ask someone to prove themselves; to challenge somebody's attempt to deceive

What happens?

A woman remembers her varied experiences with men before she married one of them. Men were 'the best and worst of times'. She held power over men who sought her attention, since she was fascinating, desirable and, above all, available, being 'footloose and fancy free'. As soon as she marries, however, she loses her tantalising power over the opposite sex. Her husband takes her for granted, all romance disappears immediately and he appears to reverse their roles and take charge in their new, married, relationship.

Structure

The lines of the first two stanzas are long and detailed, enthusiastically listing the different kinds of men the speaker knew and 'played' with before her marriage. The focus shifts with stanza three as the advantages held over the men in the game of 'courtly love' are described. The last stanza shocks the reader in its sudden contrast, the last line being cut short

Pause for thought

The words 'fluff' and 'bluff' rhyme at the end and the repeated 'uff' sound has a dull, final feel to it. Which consonant sounds, used in the earlier part of the poem, make life before marriage sound more exciting?

into only six syllables — in the same way that the pleasures of pre-marital life have been halted 'overnight'.

Occasional use of **enjambement** gives the poem a conversational feel. The pause at the end of line 12 leaves the reader waiting and wondering what she did become before the surprising next line. It is ironic that, having been a player for so long, the narrator is now reduced to an object for casual pleasure.

Internal rhymes begin with 'reach' and 'peach' (ll. 10, 11) closing the first (pre-marriage) section of the poem. The two rhyming words: 'wedded, bedded' (l. 12) are placed next to each other to make the whole procedure of marriage and its consummation sound hasty and coarse when compared to the previous romance of numerous courtships.

Note the change of pace with the last stanza. The lines are broken up by punctuation and a list of belittling names alongside that of 'wife'. '(Yes, overnight)' obviously halts the reading, but it also carries a sense of disbelief. The disappointed woman pulls the reader into her confidence as if to say 'as soon as we'd spent the night together, he no longer seemed to respect me!'

Language

Key quotation

The best and worst/ of times were men

The names the husband gives to his wife are old-fashioned, **informal** and unlikely to be welcomed by a woman. 'Little woman' is a rather demeaning name for a wife. Perhaps when originally used it seemed more humorous than its present use, where it suggests the wife is not as important as the man in the relationship. 'Bit of fluff' is even more derogatory: it links to the idea that a woman is sexually attractive, but very little else.

Other informal expressions in the last stanza combine to make the marriage seem one-sided and dominated by the husband. The word 'clicked' (l. 14) is an example of **onomatopoeia** where the sound of the physical act of the husband clicking his fingers for attention can be heard. His expectations have changed abruptly and he expects an instant response. To 'call somebody's bluff' infers you suspect you have been deceived and you challenge them to tell or show you the truth. Perhaps the husband no longer wants to play games — he's claiming his prize from his wife who is no longer 'out of reach'.

Pause for thought

Do you think Molloy could be warning women to stay 'enthroned' and unmarried?

The lengthy delights of being single and 'playing the field' are emphasised by the **repetition** of 'Men were' at the start of the first two stanzas. The repeated possessive pronoun 'my' stresses how much the speaker is in charge of her relationships. The repeated 'played' (ll. 8, 10) suggests life is a game and not to be taken seriously. To change the verb into the noun 'plaything', however, changes the mood. A wife wants to be taken seriously, to be loved, given attention and respected. She would be very unhappy to become an unimportant novelty or accessory.

'They were the rocking-horses/prancing down the promenade' (ll. 6, 7) uses **alliteration** of the plosive letter 'p' to give an impression of confident, youthful swaggering in order to show off.

Imagery

The poem relies on multiple **metaphors** for its effectiveness. You might find it helpful to refer to the glossary when analysing these. The references to medieval castles and courtly love suggest relationships based on romantic ideals and fairytales, far from the realities of real life.

Research the physical characteristics of the named animals to imagine Molloy's feelings about certain men.

Grade *booster*

The musical metaphors (ll. 7, 8) have a strong regular metre to accompany them. To boost your grade try to explain why the 'hurdy-gurdy monkey-men' and bandstand music would be exciting.

Points to consider

'The best and worst/of times were men' (ll. 2, 3) suggests that some relationships were better than others. Divide the figurative descriptions of different men into two groups. Which do you think were the narrator's favourites and which do you think she would remember and laugh about?

This poem tells a story from a female perspective. Could it be autobiographical? How much of it might be based on personal experience? There are no right or wrong answers, so you need to argue your ideas persuasively, supporting them with quotation.

Poems from the English literary heritage

'Ozymandias' by Percy Bysshe Shelley

Context

Percy Bysshe Shelley was born in Sussex in 1792. He was expelled from Oxford University, for writing a pamphlet called 'The Necessity of Atheism', attacking compulsory religion. He created a public scandal when he eloped to Scotland with 16-year-old Harriet Westbrook. While living in Ireland he made revolutionary speeches on religion and politics and wrote a political pamphlet on the French Revolution.

In 1814, Shelley eloped with another 16-year-old, Mary Godwin, and the couple travelled around Europe. By publishing his political pamphlets in Italy, it was possible to escape prosecution by the British authorities. Shelley, only 29 years old, was drowned at sea in Italy in 1822. He is known as a Romantic poet, along with Wordsworth, Coleridge, Byron and Keats.

Albo/Fotolia

Ramses II at Abu Simbel in Egypt.

Shelley had studied ancient Greek, which is probably why he chose the name 'Ozymandias', an ancient Greek version of one of Ramses II's Egyptian names. The famous Egyptian pharaoh was born around 1303 BC and is thought to have lived to be about 90 years old. He was a great warrior and commissioned numerous statues, palaces and temples to be built to symbolise his divine power, insisting that all engravings were deep so that they could not be changed. It was important to Ramses for his legacy to survive the ravages of time. The base of one sculpture reads: 'If anyone would know how great I am and where I lie, let him surpass one of my works.'

Glossary
antique (l. 1) ancient
visage (l. 4) face
pedestal (l. 9) the supporting base of a statue

What happens?

Writing in the first person, the poet begins by putting the narrative (from line 2 onwards) into the voice of a traveller, who describes the shattered remains of a great Egyptian pharaoh's statue. Although the inscription on the pedestal shows Ozymandias was a powerful, vain ruler who wished to be immortalised by the 'works' he left behind, no amount of wealth or prestige can halt the effects of time and nature. All that is left of his great empire are the desert sands.

Structure

The poem is an Italian (or Petrarchan) **sonnet**, the fourteen lines divided into eight lines (octave) and six lines (sestet), with two different rhyme patterns. This form is often chosen for love poetry, but in this case a theme of self-love leads only to thwarted ambition and decay. The **iambic pentameter** combines with the tight sonnet form to make the ironic message concise and powerful.

Shelley distances himself from the poem by putting the storytelling into the mouth of 'a traveller'. **Enjambement** is used on occasion to provide this narrative. The long middle sentence has an epic feel with its elegant, elevated language, before the sudden contrast with the scornful inscription on the pedestal (ll. 10, 11).

Language

The **imperative verbs** 'look' and 'despair', used on the inscription, are followed immediately by the statement: 'Nothing besides remains'. The irony is highlighted by the caesura that breaks up this line: a tyrannical ruler's magnificent achievements to keep his reputation immortal have been defeated by time and nature. No amount of wealth or power can protect against these.

The **irony** increases when the remaining monument to this 'king of kings' lies in pieces. Rather than glorifying the great name, the sculptor's craft has created a 'mock-up' of the face in stone to reveal the true egocentric nature of the deluded pharaoh. The 'passions' of the king are there for all to see. The word 'mock'd' is **ambiguous**, suggesting imitation of the ruler's face as well as ridicule. Ironically, the power is in the hand of the sculptor.

Alliteration is used effectively in the words 'cold command' (l. 5), the harsh consonants showing a lack of human emotions such as kindness and empathy. Again in line 13, the phrase 'boundless and bare' emphasises the endless wasteland of the Sahara desert, and the sustained 'l' sounds of 'lone and level sands' (l. 14) 'stretch' indefinitely into the distance.

The 'hand' and 'heart' of line 8 are figures of speech, where images are substituted for human attributes. The 'hand' or skill of the sculptor is able to depict the tyrant's true megalomania; the 'heart' also could be that of the sculptor, who has to indulge the king's excessive passions, ('to feed' in a Shakespearian sense can mean 'to entertain or tolerate'). His heart, in this connotation, would be the only reference to something alive and compassionate. You may, on the other hand, argue that it is Ozymandias's heart feeding his obsession for power and fame.

Shelley uses many adjectives that together demonstrate the insignificance of human power over time. They suggest great size, destruction and emptiness. None of these adjectives has anything glorious about it. Ozymandias's magnificent civilisation is reduced to two stone legs and a broken face.

Grade **booster**

Line 8: 'The hand that mock'd them and the heart that fed' is the cause of much discussion. Whose hand and whose heart are being referred to? You could boost your marks by explaining different interpretations and giving your supported opinion.

Points to consider

Shelley would not have known in 1817 that the tyrant Ramses and his ruined monuments would be featured in twentieth-century films. Have

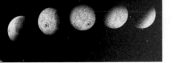

you watched disaster-style films where skyscrapers and monuments like the Statue of Liberty are buried or drowned with only their tops visible? Usually these symbolise the end of the world as we know it. Is our present-day civilisation going to disappear? Is this what the authors of the current climate debate are trying to tell us?

When this poem was first published, an English reader would most probably have seen comparisons between Ozymandias and Napoleon Bonaparte. Two years previously, the French Emperor (considered a tyrant by all his opponents), had made himself conqueror and ruler of almost all of Europe before his defeat at Waterloo in 1815 and his exile by the British on the barren island of St Helena in 1817. More recently we might think about Hitler, Stalin, Mussolini, Mao or Saddam Hussein.

It is the sculptor's art that has lasted, not the power of Ozymandias. Could Shelley be suggesting that art and language can outlast human beings and the results of their megalomania? Ironically, many people know about this pharaoh only because of this poem.

'My last Duchess' by Robert Browning

North Carolina Museum of Art/Corbis

Portrait of Lucrezia
de Medici by Agnolo
Bronzino, thought to be
Browning's 'Duchess'.

Context

Born in London in 1812, Robert Browning grew up reading the Romantic poets: Byron, Shelley and Keats. In 1846 he married Elizabeth Barrett, another English poet, and eloped with her to Italy against her father's wishes. They settled in Florence and had a son. Browning was already a celebrated poet when he died in Venice in 1889.

'My last Duchess' was first published in 1842. The Victorians were very interested (as Browning would also seem to be) in the Italian Renaissance and the way the greedy aristocracy abused its power. The poem is set in Ferrara, a city in north-east Italy. The egotistical narrator is probably based on the historical character, Alfonso II d'Este, fifth Duke of Ferrara, 1476–1534, whose first wife, 17-year-old Lucrezia de Medici, died suspiciously only three years into their marriage.

Glossary

Frà (l. 3) a friar of the Roman Catholic church

countenance (l. 7) facial expression

earnest (l. 8) serious; sincere

durst (l. 11) dared (archaic)

mantle (l. 16) a loose sleeveless coat; a cloak

officious (l. 27) interfering; too eager to offer an unwanted service

stoop (l. 34) to descend from a superior position; condescend

trifling (l. 35) frivolous behaviour

wits (l. 41) intelligence

forsooth (l. 41) in truth; indeed (archaic)

munificence (l. 49) great generosity

ample warrant (l. 50) more than sufficient guarantee or proof

just pretence (l. 50) (probably) fair claim

dowry (l. 51) money paid to a bridegroom by the bride's father

avowed (l. 52) declared

Neptune (l. 54) the god of the sea in Roman mythology

What happens?

The Duke of Ferrara proudly shows a portrait of his late wife to a Count's envoy, who has arrived to discuss the proposed marriage of the Count's daughter to the Duke. 'I call that piece a wonder, now' he tells the envoy and he relates a very unpleasant story of how his young wife even blushed seductively at the monk commissioned to paint her portrait. 'She liked whate'er/She looked on, and her looks went everywhere', he continues, listing and criticising the everyday joys that his good-natured wife had appreciated. By marrying her, he had given her his 'nine-hundred-years-old name', he explains, and yet she had no more gratitude towards him than towards anybody else who gave her an inferior gift. To confess to her that he disliked the way she smiled at everybody would require some admittance of hurt pride and jealousy, something the powerful Duke could never consider — 'I choose never to stoop,' he arrogantly exclaims. Chillingly, yet unhesitatingly, he informs the envoy that he gave 'commands' and 'all smiles stopped together'.

He is delighted by the beauty captured in the portrait, its fixed smile now controllable and hidden behind a curtain. Flattering the envoy, he immediately continues negotiations for a considerable dowry along with another wife to join his art collection.

Structure

After the one word 'Ferrara', which sets the poem firmly in the rich and influential Renaissance city, the whole poem is **one long stanza**. The

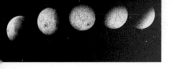

Duke's narrative does not pause sufficiently to allow any change of stanza and the lines are written in **rhyming couplets**. Frequent **enjambements** disguise the rhymes, sounding like musical, rhythmical prose, where the stresses of the **iambic pentameter** fall easily as they move across the lines:

> I call
>
> That **piece**/ a **won**/der, **now**:/Frà **Pan**/dolf's **hands**
>
> Worked **bus**/i **ly**/a **day**,/and **there**/she **stands**.

The poem only becomes congested and jerky between lines 35 and 43, where the use of many different punctuation marks chops up the narrative, giving the effect that the Duke is uncomfortable, perhaps indignant, in his attempt to explain why he had not tried to tell his young wife how he felt about her behaviour.

'Even had you skill/In speech — (which I have not) — ' the Duke argues, underestimating himself. He has skill in speech. His tone is well modulated and conversational and we never forget that he is speaking to somebody else. The poem is far from being a soliloquy, however. The reader also identifies with the envoy and can imagine and even see his responses, as clearly as if the scene were taking place on stage.

Language and imagery

The poem is a **dramatic monologue**. We listen along with the Count's messenger and work out what has happened by reading between the lines.

The Duke guesses what Frà Pandolf might have said in the form of **direct quotation**, using the word 'perhaps' (l. 15) to hint that his suspicions of seductive comments from a friar were completely unfounded. He even imagines what he could have said to his wife in direct speech (ll. 37–39) and his bluntness contrasts considerably with the gentleness of the young woman. She would appear to enjoy the natural beauty of the sunset, yet her husband's lack of finesse belittles her delight in 'the dropping of the daylight in the West'.

The **alliterative** 'd' in this phrase helps to put across his scorn and, along with the repeated 'f' in 'officious fool' (l. 27) and the plosive 'b' of 'bough' and 'broke', the reader and envoy are left in no doubt that the Duke has little respect for acts of kindness or any simple thing of beauty.

'Who'd stoop to blame/this sort of trifling?' he exclaims, the **rhetorical question** stressing his belief that he was right to put a stop to so much unnecessary gratitude. Does she not recognise the honour he has paid her? His aristocratic legacy goes back 900 years and she ought to 'rank' his gift above anybody else's.

PHILIP ALLAN LITERATURE GUIDE **FOR GCSE**

The **repetition** of some words shows the speaker's preoccupations. '…as if she were alive' he says on line 2 and again on line 47 — 'as if alive'. 'Stoop' is also used three times to highlight the Duke's obsession with rank and status. The repeated 'smile' on lines 43 and 45 angers to such an extent that 'all smiles stopped together', a **euphemism** on line 46. The Duke gives no further explanation of how he 'stopped' the smiles. He has obviously killed her, but Browning purposely leaves the reader with this open-ended shocking statement.

Key quotation

…I gave commands;

Then all smiles stopped together.

The **irony** builds as the narrative proceeds: the Duke is unaware that he is exposing his own failings. In his arrogance and vanity he creates a sympathetic image of a gentle, modest and cheerful wife. Frà Pandolf is gently ridiculed and unjustly accused of flirting with the Duchess. The Count's envoy has to suffer the detail of the Duke's increasingly frightening account, while fully aware that his master's 'fair daughter' is likely to be the next recipient of this murderer's self-obsessed expectations.

Grade **booster**

To boost your grade, examine the ambiguous possibilities of the last couplet with its feminine rhyme. Do you think the last word 'me' should be unstressed, as though the Duke is arrogantly dismissing the wealth required to commission such an expensive sculpture, or stressed to emphasise his egotism?

The envoy is regularly addressed as 'sir' to remind us of his presence, and politely but firmly instructed to 'sit' and 'rise' and 'go together down', providing a **sense of immediacy** to the drama.

Points to consider

Think about the character of the Duke. Do you think he is mad with no concept of morality or dangerously sane with a need to control?

The final lines leave the reader with a reminder that the Duke is a collector. He points out a commissioned bronze sculpture of Neptune, 'taming a sea-horse'. He can delight in beautiful things when he can control them, and the words 'thought a rarity' demonstrate his high regard for prestige. Only when a work of art is cold and dead can this man live with it, like the portrait of his 'last Duchess' that he proudly shows off — ironically the merit of it lying in its lifelike quality! The image of the powerful sea god taking control of the delicate seahorse is highly suggestive of the way he views his relationship with women.

'The river god' by Stevie Smith

Context

The poet known as Stevie Smith was born in Kingston upon Hull, Yorkshire, in 1902. Her real name was Florence Margaret Smith and she was brought up by a feminist aunt when her mother became ill and her father deserted his family by running off to sea. Common themes in her writing are death; loneliness and war; and human cruelty. A novelist as well as a poet, she never married and died of a brain tumour in 1971.

Many cultures and traditions have their own river gods and these gods, like those from Roman and Greek mythology, have their own personalities. Unlike the Christian God, who is believed to be wise and virtuous, they play tricks to achieve their own ends and demonstrate human emotions like jealousy, anger, desire and loneliness.

Some cultures have a myth where the river god demands that a sacrifice of a young maiden should be made to him each year in order for him to keep flooding the nearby land on which the people depend. The woman in each of these stories has to be beautiful, innocent and dominated by the demands of a powerful threatening male.

Ophelia by John Everett Millais, 1852.

What happens?

The poem is narrated in the persona of the river god, who reveals his many-sided personality as the poem progresses. He defends the fact that he is 'smelly' and 'old' by explaining his pleasure in the fish who live in him and the bathers who seek recreation in the water. He obviously enjoys the women bathers the most and at this point the reader maybe starts to distrust him. He goes on to describe the fun he has when people disobey the rules and drown near the weir. The last 16 lines of the poem deal with one 'beautiful lady' who drowned in the river and is still at the bottom of 'the deep river bed', held down by the weeds. He loves her and boasts about her beauty as he holds her prisoner. Nobody knows she is there and

Glossary

weir (l. 6) a low dam built across a stream to raise its level or divert its flow he delights in the secrecy, knowing she will soon have been forgotten and hoping he can keep her for himself.

Structure

Perhaps the 26 lines in one continuing stanza suggest an ever-flowing river, the shape of the river changing with its long and short lines. The voice of the river god continues without interruption in the same way that the one stanza is unbroken.

Smith's poetry rarely obeys rules. Look at the way she writes much of the poem in **rhyming couplets**. At the beginning of the poem the reader is not expecting rhymes, so the sudden almost feminine rhyme of 'women' after 'swimming' comes as a sudden shock. We were not expecting this: the first three lines were to be expected in the mouth of a river god, but suddenly there is something unsettling about the specific enjoyment of women here. Likewise the feminine rhymes of 'drowning' and 'clowning' combine cruelty and fun.

The rhyming couplets continue until line 19 when the pattern breaks with a rhetorical question, 'Oh who would guess what a beautiful white face lies there', and his emotions are exposed. There are still the **half rhymes** of 'fear', 'her', 'river' but the confidence of the earlier couplets has gone. At the end, lines 24 and 25 return to the earlier rhyming pattern before the surprise of the last line. 'If she wishes to go I will not forgive her' could seem suddenly childish and petulant or perhaps even threatening. The delights of the 'golden sleepy head' on his 'wide original bed' are left behind as he throws in this final aside, which demonstrates the vulnerability of this 'old foul river'.

Examples of **enjambement** are particularly effective.

> Waiting for me to wash away the fear
>
> She looks at me with (ll. 20, 21)

holds back the extra piece of information that the terrified woman knows she is a prisoner. The god senses this 'fear' but keeps her hostage, knowing he has the power to do so. He refuses to let her 'Go', again emphasising his refusal to release her by placing the word at the beginning of line 22. This technique is repeated with 'Now' on the next line — he has held his 'beautiful lady' for so long that she has been forgotten.

Language

Smith's choice of words is never complicated, yet often unexpected.

> So I brought her down here
>
> To be my beautiful dear

> **Key quotation**
>
> And they take a long time drowning
>
> As I throw them up now and then in the spirit of clowning.

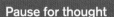

'Once there was a lady who was too bold' (l. 11) — Smith had definite feminist views and is known for writing disturbing poetry. Do you perceive that the River God might be suggesting that the lady only got what she deserved?

Pause for thought

Think about the repeated double entendre of 'river bed' where the lady lies 'with many a weed/ To hold her'. How does this make you feel?

❚❚

she writes and the word 'dear' seems initially very strange, when used by the persona of the river god, who obviously gains pleasure from tragically drowning a 'beautiful' woman. As well as suggesting somebody who is greatly loved, there is also the connotation that she will pay 'dearly' for staying in his 'deep river bed'. The adverb 'merrily' on line 9 is also unusual. It fits with the 'spirit of clowning', but becomes sinister when the following line states he has 'plenty of go', a phrase implying lots of energy, but also hints at sexual innuendo.

The **conversational tone** throws in the **interjection** 'Oh' three times, along with 'so' (l. 13) and 'They say' (l. 23), which give the impression of a shared confidence with the reader.

The regular rhythm and balanced halves of the first two lines create a comfortable mood at the start. The **alliterative letters** 'l' and 'p' set the scene and the 'fish float by' in line 3 to add to the expected description of an established kindly river. But suddenly the tone turns threatening. If the people bathing disobey the rules and get into difficulties, then he turns violent and even sadistic. He comments that the 'fools…take a long time drowning' and delights in their distress.

When he describes the drowning of one particular 'lady' (l. 11), his tone changes again and he appears capable of gentleness and loving. There is **repetition** in the line 'Oh will she stay with me will she stay' and a sense of yearning and even doubt that he will have the power to keep her. He is obviously preoccupied by the loveliness of the dead woman as he repeats the word 'beautiful' four times. With the **rhetorical question** on line 19 he seems to be gloating that he has a secret.

Grade *booster* ❗

…merrily I flow,

O I may be an old foul river but I have plenty of go.

Write about the **assonance** of the repeated 'o' sound here to raise your marks. Does the river god sound boastful, threatening or teasing? Lines 5/6, also lines 17/18, use repeated vowel sounds for special effects.

Points to consider

In Shakespeare's tragedy *Hamlet*, Hamlet's girlfriend, Ophelia, drowns in a brook and is found floating in the water. Perhaps the lady waiting 'with her golden sleepy head' conjures up an image similar to John Everett Millais' depiction of a beautiful Ophelia in his famous painting.

Although Smith died in 1971 there are personality traits in the river god's persona similar to criminals in the twenty-first century. Read lines 20 and 21. Think of cases where girls have been abducted and imprisoned for many years at the mercy of a cruel captor, who believes he alone can be the carer and saviour of the victim. Does line 22 remind you of children who have been kidnapped and never found?

'The hunchback in the park' by Dylan Thomas

Context

Dylan Thomas was born in Swansea, South Wales, in 1914. He left school at seventeen to work as a newspaper reporter, before moving to London three years later in 1934, the same year that he published his first book of poetry. He married a dancer, Caitlin MacNamara, and returned to Wales in 1937, where they rented a cottage in Laugharne, Carmarthenshire and had three children.

Despite a stormy marriage and heavy drinking, Thomas became a very popular speaker, making broadcasts for BBC radio and giving lecture tours in the USA. He died in 1953, at the young age of 39, due to alcohol abuse.

Cwmdonkin Park in Swansea, the setting for 'The hunchback in the park', is close to where Dylan Thomas grew up. Often writing about his past as a boy, he remembers his childhood adventures in this poem and the characters that frequented the park.

In his radio broadcast 'Reminiscences of Childhood' he describes the park:

> A world within the world of the sea town…full of terrors and treasures…a country just born and always changing…and that park grew up with me… In that small, iron-railed universe of rockery, gravel-path, playbank, bowling-green, bandstand, reservoir, chrysanthemum garden…in the grass one must keep off, I endured, with pleasure, the first agonies of unrequited love…

Glossary

hunchback (ll. 1, 41 and title) a person whose back is hunched due to abnormal convex curvature of the upper spine. The word 'hunchback' is not an acceptable word to use for a disabled person, but this is the word the children used when Dylan Thomas was a boy

sombre (l. 6) gloomy, sad

groves (l. 30) groups of cultivated trees

What happens?

The poem describes the lonely, homeless man with a hunched back who spends every day in the park. He is taunted by local youths who use the park as an adventure playground. In his own imagination he visualises a woman with no deformity who can stand 'straight and tall' all night in the park, when he has to leave and return to his dog kennel where he sleeps.

Structure

Written in seven six-line stanzas, each stanza moves the description along: the park is unlocked in the morning, the day progresses and then the park is once again locked up for the night. The **rhymes** 'park' and 'dark' of stanza one are repeated in the last stanza, enforcing the cyclical nature of day and night. Stanzas two, three and four also have a pair of perfect rhymes; stanzas five and six, however, leave all rhyming behind in the freedom of the imagination, whether that of the 'wild boys' or the homeless man.

The third stanza has a **musical rhythm**, the second and fourth lines rhyming to create an overall effect of accepted routine. Stanza four uses the **feminine rhymes** of 'rockery' and 'mockery', a form of rhyme often used for comic effect, but in this poem the humour is enjoyed only by those who imitate the man's disability. Elsewhere Thomas relies on **half rhyme** to present the musicality of the poem — 'water/enter', 'gravel/kennel', etc.

Absence of punctuation, except for three full stops, also keeps the poem moving though the day. Does Thomas decide to use full stops for specific reasons? Perhaps he throws in a strong personal opinion, changes the tone, or closes the poem?

Lines 36 and 38–40 list the impressions the 'hunchback' takes away with him from the park each day. His mind is full of beauty and space and the lack of commas in the list merges the memories into one.

Language

The hunchbacked man returns each day to the same park and this routine is presented by the **repetition** of words.

There is also a great deal of **contrast** in the poem:

- the trees in the park are graceful like the swans; the birds have the freedom of the air; the lake water is calming. The hunchbacked man, on the other hand, has limited freedom: he is locked into his body in the way the park is locked up
- chains are tied around the park gates each night; the drinking cup is chained to the water fountain, yet the poet's voice insists that the

---

Pause for thought

The lack of punctuation and the use of enjambement give the poem a timeless feeling. Do you think Thomas looks back on his childhood and remembers these times with nostalgia? Adults often say that their childhood days seemed long and endless.

PHILIP ALLAN LITERATURE GUIDE **FOR GCSE**

'hunchback' is not chained to his kennel in the way a dog would probably be

- the Sunday church bell rings out in a 'sombre' way as the park is closed; when it is open the 'wild boys' shout, laugh and roar as they play their imaginary childhood games
- the 'hunchback' is 'alone' (l. 26) and 'solitary' (l. 2), whereas the children arrive, play in groups and leave together
- the 'woman figure' imagined by the hunchbacked man is 'straight and tall' in comparison to his 'crooked bones'.

The woman figure is also 'a figure without fault', the sustained 'f' sound making her seem perfect in form and beauty. The poem uses other examples of **alliteration**: the 'Sunday sombre bell' tolls; 'the truant boys from the town' is a rhythmical mischievous phrase; 'roar on the rockery stones' alliterates the 'r' and uses **onomatopoeia** to suggest the sound of tigers.

The **tone** of the poem changes when the 'boys from the town' enter the park and begin to shout — 'Hey mister' on line 15. They bring excitement, agility and the cruelty of insensitive 'mockery' into the park and the poem. The earlier stanzas have described the quiet loneliness of the homeless man, but suddenly the exuberance of youth breaks the stillness. At the end of the day the silence returns to the locked park.

Imagery

Used **metaphorically** on line 3, 'propped' gives the idea that the 'trees and water' sustain the lonely man. He needs to walk in the wide open spaces, away from the built-up city.

> **Key quotation**
>
> Like the park birds he came early
>
> Like the water he sat down

When the park is unlocked it 'lets the trees and water enter'. Instead of people entering the park, the **personified** rural space becomes a part of its visitors' day. It moves into their minds and gives them nature's space to breathe.

'The loud zoo of the willow groves' (l. 22) is the first animal metaphor. The small group of trees suddenly becomes alive with the screams and calls of the uninhibited 'wild boys'. They make 'tigers jump out of their eyes' on line 28 as they 'roar' and play their games, set in dangerous and exotic places. The city of Swansea was a busy port and the boys would be used to seeing sailors. The groves of the park provided exciting, mysterious places to imagine foreign adventures. Do the woods become the sea in the shadows of the trees when they are 'blue with sailors'?

Grade *booster*

Why do you think the park is 'unmade' (l. 37) during the night when it is locked up? Contrast the boys who '*made* tigers jump out of their eyes' and the hunchbacked man who '*made*…A woman figure without fault'.

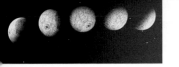

The two **similes** on lines 13 and 14 compare the homeless man to creatures of nature and the natural elements. In a similar way 'the wild boys' are 'innocent as strawberries' despite their taunting.

Points to consider

On line 10 the poet places himself in the poem, 'the fountain basin where I sailed my ship', recreating a moment from his own childhood. Do you think he identifies with the 'truant boys from the town' or remains an observer? How does he feel about the 'old dog sleeper' and the 'mockery'?

'The ruined maid' by Thomas Hardy

Context

Thomas Hardy was born in 1840 near the town of Dorchester in Dorset. After the success of *Far From the Madding Crowd* in 1874, in which he created an imaginary world called Wessex, based on Dorset and its surrounding counties, he turned to writing full-time.

From 1888 Hardy was attempting to write more realistically about the struggles between people from different social classes and the hypocrisy of Victorian morality. His frankness created problems with editors who were concerned about the shocked public's reaction to his books, particularly *Tess of the D'Urbervilles* and *Jude the Obscure*, both of which examined 'fallen women', sex, the class system and attitudes to marriage. Distressed by this response to his novels, Hardy began to concentrate on plays and poetry. He died in 1928 and was buried in Poets' Corner, Westminster Abbey.

'The ruined maid' was written in 1866 but not published until 1901 in Hardy's collection *Poems of the Past and Present*.

Glossary

'Melia (l. 1) Amelia

spudding up docks (l. 6) digging up weeds

gay (l. 7) brightly coloured

barton (l. 9) farm

thik oon; theas oon (l. 10) that one; this one

'ee (l. 11) thee (you)

hag-ridden dream (l. 17) tormented nightmare

sock (l. 18) hit, strike, punch

megrims (l. 19) migraine headaches

melancholy (l. 19) sadness

What happens?

The poem is a dramatic dialogue between two young women who meet up in town, having known each other previously when they were both country girls working on a farm and living poor harsh lives. The first unnamed speaker is amazed to see the second young woman, 'Melia, looking so finely dressed and questions her new-found 'prosper-ity'. 'Melia tells her it is because she has been 'ruined', a derogatory word used by high-minded Victorians for girls and women who had consented to unmarried sexual liaisons and were living as mistresses or prostitutes.

Even 'Melia's speech has become more refined, and she continues to inform her previous acquaintance that there are definite advantages to being 'ruined': there is no hard physical work to do and 'one's pretty lively'. She concludes by telling the other young woman that ironically 'a raw country girl' could never enjoy her envied lifestyle, since she 'ain't ruined'.

Working class girls in Victorian times had few opportunities for improving their lives. Higher education was denied them. Moral values for men were different. If a man wanted to take a mistress, it was not frowned upon in the same way that a woman who sacrificed her honour would be considered immoral and undeserving of respect, help and sympathy. 'The ruined maid' is a satire, in which Hardy uses irony and mocks Victorian attitudes towards 'fallen women' by depicting possible contrasting situations. The clean-living girl has a miserable poverty-stricken life, whereas the 'ruined maid', contented with her choice, seems to have improved her quality of life.

> **Key quotation**
>
> 'One's pretty lively when ruined,' said she.

Structure

'The ruined maid' is often described as being in **ballad form**, because of its song-like narrative, four-lined stanzas with a fourth line refrain, and lively dialogue. The aabb **rhyme pattern** combines with **strong metre** in the eleven- (or occasionally twelve-) syllable lines, each consisting of four metric feet. After an iambic foot (dee dum or unstressed, stressed) the remaining three feet are anapaestic in most lines (dee dee dum or unstressed, unstressed, stressed); lines 6, 15, 18 and 22 have four anapaestic feet.

> **Pause for thought**
>
> Examine the way the anapaestic metre places the stress on final syllables in words such as 'prosper-ity', 'compa-ny', 'la-dy', 'melancho-ly'. Do these words, when made into awkward –ee rhymes, suggest the vulgarity of the speaker — or do they show she is trying to speak above her status?

— You **left**/us in **tat**/ters, with **out**/shoes or **socks**,

Tired of **digg**/ing po **ta**/toes and **spudd**/ing up **docks**;

Together the rhyme and metre, ideal techniques for irony and comedy, give a light-heartedness to the poem.

Unlike the previous stanzas, 'Melia's final retort is given two lines. 'My dear —' she directly addresses her previous acquaintance, repeating the endearment used to address herself in the first line. The last line, with its central break for effect, changes the metre to put emphasis on the important word 'You' in the whole statement 'You ain't ruined'. The tables are turned and the prostitute is now judging the 'raw country girl', leaving the reader to consider the dubious but attractive benefits of the ruined

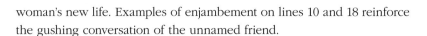

woman's new life. Examples of enjambement on lines 10 and 18 reinforce the gushing conversation of the unnamed friend.

Language

The fourth line of each stanza provides 'Melia's sarcastic reply. In this ironic **refrain** she always uses the word 'ruined' to stress the derogatory term given to women whose moral reputation is ruined. Her contrasting appearance, of course, suggests that her situation has improved considerably and the reader questions which of the two women has the harder life. Is Hardy commenting on the injustice of Victorian morality?

Use of the Dorset **dialect** contrasts the speech of the first speaker with 'Melia, who has learned a more refined way of speaking. The country girl speaks of 'docks', 'thik oon', 'theas oon' — and exclaims 'Your talking quite fits 'ee for high compa-ny!' Hardy allows the vain, confident 'Melia's previous dialect to creep in on the last line, however, when her true humble origins are revealed: '"You ain't ruined," said she.'

The bouncy rhythm is helped along by **alliteration**. The repeated 'b' sound in line 7 describes amazement at 'Melia's colourful appearance, a distinct change from her 'face blue and bleak' when she suffered the cold, harsh working conditions of the farm. At home she would 'sigh' and 'sock' about her disadvantaged lifestyle, and complain of 'megrims or melancho-ly', the sustained letters 's' and 'm' effective for describing her dreary mood.

Imagery

'Your hands were like paws then' is an animal-themed **simile** where the rough, swollen hands of the farm girl resembled thick paws. In contrast her hands are now slim, fitting into elegant gloves, and no longer required to do hard physical labour.

'Melia's home life before she turned to prostitution is **metaphorically** described as 'a hag-ridden dream', probably riddled with apprehension, due to poverty. The chances of a working-class girl gaining social elevation were the stuff that only dreams were made of and rarely could become a reality. 'Melia chose to sacrifice her morality in order to live the lifestyle of the wealthier classes.

Ideas to consider

The Latin word 'melior' means better. It is interesting that Hardy chooses the name 'Melia (a shortened form of Amelia) for the woman who appears to have 'bettered' her situation. Hardy once called himself a 'meliorist', that is, someone who believes that society can be improved by people making an effort.

'Melia's material wealth, of course, can only be temporary and will disappear as time destroys her youth and beauty. With the reputation of a disreputable woman, her future will probably be bleak. Then she will realise the full meaning of what it is to be 'ruined'.

'Casehistory: Alison (head injury)' by U. A. Fanthorpe

Context

Ursula Askham Fanthorpe was born in Kent in 1929. She worked as an English teacher for 16 years, before deciding she needed a change and taking an administrative job in a Bristol neurological hospital. Here she met men and women with terrible injuries and conditions. She admits she found it 'moving, horrifying and beautiful' and started to write poems, including 'Casehistory: Alison' in the personas of some of these patients, many of whom were not able to speak for themselves. Having access to the patients' case histories, Fanshawe recognised how clinical, cold and uncompassionate the hospital records were and was inspired to write about the 'strange specialness' of people like Alison.

Side Effects, published in 1978, was the first of nine poetry collections. In 2001, Fanthorpe was awarded a CBE for services to poetry and received the Queen's Gold Medal for Poetry in 2003. She died in April 2009, aged 79.

Glossary
enmeshed (l. 4) caught up (trapped) as though in a net
autocratic (l. 6) bossy and domineering
Degas (l. 7) French artist, 1834–1917, well known for painting ballet dancers
lugs (l. 9) drags or hauls with difficulty
consistency (l. 19) keeping things the same in a harmonious way
assert (l. 23) declare; insist upon

What happens?

The dramatic monologue is spoken in the voice of Alison, a head injury patient. Fanthorpe imagines what she would say if she were to look at a photograph of her healthy former self.

Structure

Written in nine three-lined stanzas, the poem has a very regular shape. Most stanzas, all in free verse, are composed of two six-syllable lines either side of a longer, eleven-syllable, line.

The first and last stanzas are slightly different, however, the third line having only five single-syllable words. Line 3, 'A bright girl she was', repeated in a separated line at the end of the poem, is dramatic and poignant in its simplicity. 'I am her future' (l. 27) is also memorable when Alison understands that the girl in the photo could never have known the sad events of her future.

Some lines use **enjambement** to create a particular effect: the natural pause at the end of line 4 gives extra emphasis to 'Fat', the first word of line 5. Lines 9/10 and 14/15 use this same technique.

Language

Alison's head injury has resulted in a complete change of personality. Examine the **contrasts** before and after the event or accident that caused the injury.

- The pre-accident Alison was 'bright' with 'delicate angles' and 'poise'. Now she is overweight and struggles to climb stairs. (The brain is responsible for starting movement in all parts of the body and also for co-ordinating movements to make them smooth and graceful.)
- She achieved well at school and went into a job with promising career prospects that demanded intelligence and taking responsibility. Now she can only be 'proud of this younger self' and rely on hospitalised care.
- She can remember very little of her past life and, because she has no short-term memory, she needs 'reminding every morning'. Along with her memory loss, her thinking processes have been damaged and she cannot process information:

I should like to keep faith with her lack of faith,

But forget her reasons.

Fanthorpe uses **repetition**. 'A bright girl she was' (ll. 3, 28) highlights the sad difference between the intelligent young woman with a future to look forward to and the head injury patient who has become 'her future'. The word 'smile' is used four times in stanzas 4 and 5 — the injured Alison has forgotten what there was to smile about. 'I should like to keep faith with her lack of faith' — she no longer has the reasoning skills to work out what she believes.

Loss of memory would appear to be the greatest concern for Alison, all the more disconcerting since she is sufficiently aware that she 'shall never get over what (she does) not remember' (ll. 17, 18). Words connected to the theme of forgetfulness are scattered through the middle stanzas: 'forgotten', 'reminding', 'remember', 'forget'.

PHILIP ALLAN LITERATURE GUIDE **FOR GCSE**

Imagery

The metaphor 'Enmeshed in comforting/Fat' reminds the reader that the 'bright' Alison has been trapped inside her injured self. Damage to her brain has probably reduced her mobility, co-ordination and motivation and drugs given to head injury patients often result in excess weight gain.

Another effective metaphor describes the face in the photo as 'broken/By nothing sharper than smiles' (ll. 10, 11). Does this suggest that the radiant face shows no fear for the future? She would seem to be free of all anxiety and cannot possibly know what lies ahead. Even the grieving process is manageable when a person can remember, adjust and move on — 'She has digested/Mourning' in the photograph.

> Her autocratic knee
>
> Like a Degas dancer's
>
> Adjusts to the observer with airy poise,

The only **simile** in the poem compares the youthful 'poise' of the girl in the photograph to the woman who can now barely drag herself upstairs. A ballet dancer's knee sometimes has to bear the weight of the whole body in repeated jumps, bends and twists. The girl in the photo appears to have perfect balance and control, her 'autocratic knee' directing her movements.

Pause for thought

Why do you think 'Consistency matters'? The injured Alison would probably want to keep things the same. For people with loss of memory it is also important that each day is made up of routines. How often do you think Alison looks at the photograph?

Ideas to consider

How do you think Alison knows she has a husband, that she is her mother's 'only daughter', that she has A-levels and had a good job? Perhaps Fanthorpe is telling us this through Alison's voice so that we can explore Alison's feeling with her. Do you consider that knowing this but remembering very little else would be worse than having no understanding at all of her condition?

Fanthorpe explained why she wrote this poem and another called 'Casehistory: Julie (encephalitis)': 'Neuropsychiatric disorders were new to me, and I felt the urge to tell the world.

A ballerina painted by Degas.

TopFoto

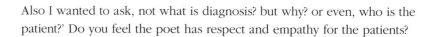

Also I wanted to ask, not what is diagnosis? but why? or even, who is the patient?' Do you feel the poet has respect and empathy for the patients?

'On a portrait of a deaf man' by John Betjeman

Context

John Betjeman was born in 1906 in North London and was the only child of Ernest and Mabel Betjemann. In 1909, the family moved to West Hill in Highgate, only half a mile away, but a more affluent area. His school holidays were spent at Trebetherick in Cornwall, where the family owned property. Although he attended Oxford University, he did not complete his degree course, but taught for a while, edited an architectural magazine and wrote guide books. He is well known for his light, satirical poetry, but he also revealed a great deal of himself and his autobiographical details in some of his poems. Awarded a CBE in 1960 and knighted in 1969, he became Poet Laureate in 1972. Betjeman's love of Cornwall lasted all his life and he was buried there when he died in 1984.

It was well known that Betjeman did not have a comfortable adult relationship with his father, who had hoped his son would follow him into the furniture-making trade. John preferred poetry and literature and, after his father's death, remembered his father with definite affection, contrasting his memories of his 'kind' deaf father with his own fear of death and its gruesome finality in 'Portrait of a deaf man'.

Glossary

discreetly (l. 2)
modestly; not showily

shroud (l. 4) a cloth to wrap around a corpse

Carrara-covered (l. 23) covered with white marble headstones

What happens?

The poem is an unusual elegy, detailing the father's likes and dislikes in a warm, affectionate way, yet juxtaposing (placing two ideas next to each other for contrast) these earthly pleasures with macabre, horror-filled descriptions of imagined bodily decay. At the end of the poem Betjeman questions his religious beliefs. At this time in his life his agnosticism has led him to an obsession with death and its finality and he is unable to gain nostalgic comfort from fond memories of his father. He can no longer believe in a deserved afterlife offered by his previous High Anglican faith.

Pause for thought

Could Betjeman be writing this poem with such tight control over the rhyme and metre because he cannot control death or his own fear of death? At least he knows that, although he cannot be immortal, his poetry can live on.

Structure

The poem is written in eight regular four-lined stanzas. The abcb rhyme scheme fits the ballad metre where the first and third eight-syllable lines are in iambic tetrameter (four feet with the second syllable stressed) and the second and fourth six-syllable lines in iambic trimester (three feet with the second syllable stressed). This jaunty rhythm appears light and easy at the start of each stanza, suddenly shocking the reader with its unexpectedly gruesome content in the second half.

Language

The first two stanzas would appear, on first reading, to be written in the third person. Line 9: 'He took me on long silent walks' suddenly changes into a first-person narrative, continuing into stanza four where the poet expresses his personal fears: 'I do not like to think/Of maggots in his eyes'. The next three stanzas then return to third-person description, before the sudden change in the last stanza, when God is addressed directly.

'You, God,' Betjeman challenges. 'You ask me to believe You.'

Ending the poem in the second person, using the pronoun 'You' for God, leaves behind the elegy to his father and places new emphasis on his religious doubts. He once said: 'I hang on to my faith by my eyelids. A lot of the time, I think it is all rot.' When he wrote this poem he obviously could 'only see decay'.

We gain a full appreciation of life through our senses. Betjeman's father was stone-deaf, but his son celebrates the use of his other senses as the poem progresses:

- Stanza one introduces the **visual appearance** of the 'kind old face' and 'the egg-shaped head'.
- Stanza two selects **taste** and his father's love of dining out in the City and eating 'potatoes in their skin'.
- Stanza three reverses the sense of **sound** to describe the father's soundless world of 'long silent walks' where the birdsong could not be heard.
- Stanza five evokes the country **smells** of 'Cornish air', 'ploughed-up soil' and the linseed oil and turpentine of oil painting.
- Stanzas six and seven deal with the **tactile** (touch) images of cold white marble and shaking 'hands with many friends'.

The description of his father through sensory detail makes the contrasting grotesque thoughts on the decomposition of his father's corpse even more horrific.

When describing his father when alive, the lines are written in the **past tense**; when dead, the **present tense**

> **Key quotation**
>
> And when he could not hear me speak
>
> He smiled and looked so wise

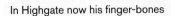

Grade **booster**

In Highgate now his finger-bones

Stick through his finger-ends.

These lines are almost comical in their grotesqueness. To make your response analytical, write about the way people sometimes cope with their fear and dismay by joking about harsh truths.

is used to highlight the poet's preoccupation with the ongoing process of decomposition. The last stanza leaps into the present tense as Betjeman declares that he is expected to continue in the present with hopes for the future, but cannot.

The **oxymoron** 'discreetly loud' suggests that, although his father wanted colour and perhaps to show he was quite fashionable, nevertheless he did not want to attract attention to himself. Only a close friend or relative could appreciate this characteristic.

Another technique used effectively is the **alliterative** line 22: 'Which hangs on Highgate Hill'. The verb 'hangs' conjures up the macabre image of executions and Highgate cemetery is a huge Victorian graveyard, full of Gothic tombs and monuments. Ernest Betjemann was buried here despite his dislike of 'that place'.

Ideas to consider

Do you think Betjeman struggled to write an elegy that simply praised his father's character, since he was too upset to write simple truths? Writing to his father in 1929 he wrote: 'Often most serious feelings are expressed in a joke. I very rarely talk about what I really feel.' Or was he really examining his lack of religious faith?

Although Betjeman seems to have had a good relationship with his father when he was a child, they did not always agree when the poet was an adult. Could the word 'deaf' in the poem's title suggest a lack of understanding and reduced communication as well as its literal meaning?

Place

Contemporary poems

'The blackbird of Glanmore' by Seamus Heaney

Context

Seamus Heaney was born in 1939 in Northern Ireland and has always thought of himself as Irish rather than British. Since his first book of poetry, *Death of a Naturalist*, was published in 1966, he has become a famous and greatly admired contemporary poet. Although he has shown concern for the political problems he has lived through in Ireland, he still writes from a personal and thoughtful viewpoint. Much of his poetry describes his love of nature and his childhood roots where he grew up as the eldest of nine children on the family farm in County Derry. In 1995 he won the Nobel Prize for literature.

'The blackbird of Glanmore' (which Heaney says is his favourite poem), is from his collection *District and Circle*, winner of the 2006 T. S. Eliot Prize. Forty years previously Heaney had written a poem called 'Mid-term break' where he describes a very sad family event. He is called home from boarding school when his four-year-old brother, Christopher, has been killed in a car accident. This is the 'lost brother' he remembers and affectionately refers to in this poem:

> No gaudy scars, the bumper knocked him clear.

> A four foot box, a foot for every year.

In country folklore, myths and superstitions, black birds, particularly crows, rooks and ravens, are often linked to the arrival of life or death. In Norse folk tales, when they perch on roofs they are considered omens of death for the cursed family below. Other cultures believe that a human soul, once freed from the body, takes the form of a bird.

What happens?

Heaney describes a time when he arrives home and sees a blackbird on the grass. He remembers a neighbour's story of how a blackbird had sat on the shed roof of his family home for weeks before his young brother had been tragically killed. He recognises comparisons between his little brother, excited to see him home from school, and the starts and stills of the cheeky, nervy bird.

Glossary

cavorting (l. 16)
prancing about in a lively, boisterous way

hedge-hop (l. 31) to fly close to the ground

absolute (l. 31)
complete; free from any doubts or limitations

Key quotation

And I think of one gone to him,

A little stillness dancer —

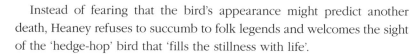

Instead of fearing that the bird's appearance might predict another death, Heaney refuses to succumb to folk legends and welcomes the sight of the 'hedge-hop' bird that 'fills the stillness with life'.

Structure

Written in six stanzas, each of six lines, the final line is always separated from the rest of the stanza. This gives the sixth line particular emphasis. Look at the strength of feeling of line 6: 'It's you, blackbird, I love.' In other stanzas the fifth line is held by enjambement as well as the space before the final line. The neighbour waits with a pause at the end of line 23, before adding her own suspicions: 'But I never liked yon bird'; the 'shortlived' panic of the bird and 'shadow on raked gravel' may be temporary but Heaney waits before exclaiming 'In front of my house of life.'

There are also pauses (or caesuras) within lines. Line 7: 'I park, pause, take heed./Breathe. Just breathe' slows down the reading to provide an image of the poet watching and waiting in the stillness of the moment, remembering how a blackbird was connected to his little brother's death many years previously. Re-read stanzas five and six to appreciate the effect of other mid-line pauses.

Language

The first stanza has a musical quality like very old English poetry. Examine the way certain sustained consonants such as 'r', 'l', and 'v' are used. This is called **consonance** and there are also examples of **alliteration**. The plosive 'p' in 'park, pause', for example, halts the reading for a short time in the way the poet stops the car. Stanza five combines the techniques of **onomatopoeia** and alliterative use of the sharp letters 'c' and 't' to reproduce the blackbird's call of alarm (which sounds like a rattle), following the 'clunk' of the gate lock.

The second line uses an **oxymoron**: 'Filling the stillness with life'. There are echoes here of a still-life picture yet the bird adds realism by its presence. A similar effect is gained by 'little stillness dancer' (l. 14), a 'cavorting' little boy whose life was stilled when he was so young.

> ### Pause for thought
>
> 'The house of death' becomes 'the house of life', two metaphors describing the poet's changing emotions. Do you think the 'lone, clay roof' could suggest the cold, dark earth above a coffin?

The **assonant** 'ee' sound of 'heed' (l. 7) and the **repeated** word 'breathe' on line 8 cause the reader to slow down and take a moment with the poet to 'sit' and reflect. Lines 1 and 5 are also repeated at the end of the poem. These lines can be understood literally — the blackbird 'on the grass' flies only a short distance towards the ivy-covered house when disturbed. The nature of the differing vegetation, however, is worth considering. Whereas grass is bright, fresh and in the open, ivy is darker, funereal and secretive. Life arrives and death departs.

The conflict between life and death is evident throughout the poem. Language connected with death is interspersed with 'living' vocabulary. Heaney seems to be contemplating the sad loss of a loved brother while embracing the short delights of life.

Creating **compound words** such as 'haunter-son' and 'hedge-hop' is a poetic way of condensing more than one idea into a single word. Memories of the lost son and brother still keep the child alive and the name 'hedge-hop' is an endearing name for a bird that lives and flies so close to the ground.

Stanza four **quotes** the words of a neighbour directly to emphasise the extent of the superstition attached to the sighting of a black bird close to a death. Heaney also remembers lines he once translated (probably from Anglo-Saxon into English) in lines 10–12. In line 31 he addresses the blackbird by declaring: 'I am absolute/ For you'. In Act III of Shakespeare's *Measure for Measure* a young man condemned to death is advised: 'Be absolute for death; either death or life/Shall thereby be the sweeter.' (If you can approach death without fear, then it will make your life better.) Do you feel Heaney has decided by the end of the poem to celebrate life — even though life is short and unpredictable?

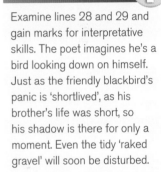

Grade **booster**

Examine lines 28 and 29 and gain marks for interpretative skills. The poet imagines he's a bird looking down on himself. Just as the friendly blackbird's panic is 'shortlived', as his brother's life was short, so his shadow is there for only a moment. Even the tidy 'raked gravel' will soon be disturbed.

Ideas to consider

Seamus Heaney's love of nature is evident in much of his poetry. In the last stanza of this poem he expresses his delight in the 'picky, nervy goldbeak'. To appreciate the detailed description it is helpful to know the movements of a blackbird. The site www.bbc.co.uk/nature/species/Common_Blackbird shows the close-up movements of this alert, watchful songster, who seems to answer back in short, cheeky bursts of 'ready talkback'.

When Heaney writes: 'It's you, blackbird, I love' he seems to be thinking of his brother. How many words and phrases in the poem can you find that could refer both to the little boy and the blackbird?

'A vision' by Simon Armitage

Context

For information on Simon Armitage, see 'The clown punk' on page 7. 'A vision' is from the collection *Tyrannosaurus Rex versus the Corduroy Kid*, published in 2006.

Pause for thought

Over the last few decades, technology has improved rapidly and detailed construction has been increasingly designed in computer-aided design systems. How can this change the outcome of architects' proposals?

What happens?

Armitage describes the ambitious and somewhat fanciful plans that town planners once had to turn towns into futuristic Utopias. Blueprints showed 'cities like *dreams*' where the citizens lived clean, neat, ordered lives. Years later, the poet tells how he pulled such unrealised plans from a 'landfill site'. He is probably suggesting that such a vision was always impractical and unlikely to happen, that people's dreams of the future are just as unlikely to materialise as the 'artists' impressions' of 'a beautiful place'.

Structure

The poem is written is five four-lined stanzas of free verse. The first line makes an immediate statement, placing emphasis on the final word — 'once' — an instant clue to the poet's disillusionment. Frequent use of **enjambement** gives a conversational feel, line 12 running across a stanza break to surprise with 'electric cars' (an exciting but impractical concept). The poem's focus shifts for the final stanza. After the description of the envisaged prototype town, the poet himself enters the poem to explain what happened to such ambitious yet unrealistic plans.

Language

The **alliterative** use of the letter 'b' in stanza one puts excitement into the vision of the future. This continues into stanza two where numerous **sibilant** 's' sounds give a sense of fashionable luxury to the sketches of 'smoked glass' and 'tubular steel'. There is also a touch of smugness in the 'model drivers, motoring home'.

Armitage prompts 'Remember' at the beginning of line 2 and this imperative verb pulls the reader straight into the poem. Line 9 begins 'And people like us', a similar direct appeal to bring us into the experience.

The **repetition** of 'or' (ll. 10, 12, 13) has the interesting effect of presenting a list as though it is being spontaneously remembered.

A theme of playing games runs through the poem. Could this be because Armitage feels such plans were always practically unsound and not possible financially — that those in authority were never aware of people's realistic needs?

- 'Board-game suburbs' presents an image of the neat little plastic houses and hotels used in the game of Monopoly, bought with fake money by the rich players.
- 'Executive toys' are useless novelty gadgets intended to sit on the desk of people who make important company decisions
- 'Fuzzy-felt' is the name of a young child's creative play game. Pre-cut shapes made very unrealistic pictures and grass has to be long bright green pieces of felt.

Imagery

The poem uses the **metaphor** of the town's abandoned plans to suggest that a Utopian future is not possible for the society in which we live. Think of today's problems with crime, pollution, traffic congestion, inadequate housing — none of these is considered when the original blueprints are put together, therefore dreams of a beautiful place to live are unlikely to come true.

'Cantilevered by light' is a striking **metaphor** as well. Does this project an image of our dream cities being held up in our imaginations, stretching out into glowing futures? Perhaps you link the italic *'dreams'* to the idea that they can never become real — that the plans end up with no support: they are 'up in the air' or they 'disappear into thin air' or they are even 'riding the air' (l. 19)?

There are two **similes** on lines 6, 7 and 8. One of these: 'Modes of transportation/like fairground rides or executive toys', conjures up pictures of big dippers, big wheels, runaway trains and perhaps Newton's Cradle, the most famous executive toy. Find photos of funfair rides and executive toys to help you imagine what the architects of the new towns had in mind.

Ideas to consider

A reviewer of Simon Armitage's collection of poetry that includes this poem suggests that Armitage's disillusionment is due to the fact that he had reached middle age when he wrote 'A vision'. Most young people are positive about what their future holds. Do you think your future will feel 'unlived in' when you get older? Is the future not always 'a beautiful place' that contrasts with the present?

Grade *booster*

'Cities like dreams' is a key image of the poem. Read line 8 aloud: 'Cities like dreams, cantilevered by light.' Can you perceive and write about the wishful tone created by the long assonant 'i' and 'ee' sounds?

Key quotation

I pulled that future out of the north wind

At the landfill site,

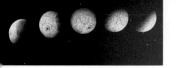

Find out about examples of effective architecture where lives have been transformed, for example: 'Urban Splash' projects; the South Bank area in central London; Salford Quays, Manchester; and many other regeneration projects around the country. How do you think Simon Armitage would respond if you questioned him about the plans for new building projects in your area?

'The moment' by Margaret Atwood

Context

Margaret Atwood, successful Canadian novelist and poet, was born in 1939. She grew up in Toronto, but spent her summers in the Canadian wilderness of Northern Quebec, accompanying her father, who studied forest insects. She has strong views on environmental issues and is a member of the Canadian Green party. 'The moment' was written in 1976.

What happens?

The poem begins by looking at human endeavour and achievement, which can lead to a sense of deserved ownership, whether of a house, land, colony or country. The second stanza shocks us by detailing the earth's gradual removal of its essential resources, beginning with a gentle withdrawal, through catastrophe to eventual apocalypse. The final stanza reminds us, in the voice of the earth, that we are short-lived 'visitors' to our planet and all attempts to explore and claim land, to proclaim ownership, are futile. It is 'the other way round': the earth sustains us and ultimately has control of the future of the human race. Written in 1976, the poet was fully aware of contemporary themes of earth management on both a personal and universal level.

Key quotation

We never belonged to you.

Structure

The first two stanzas are constructed of one long sentence. The **enjambement** between these stanzas 'is the same moment' when the poem turns 'the other way round' and surprises the reader by reversing the whole idea of ownership. The pause after '*I own this*', therefore, has a particularly dramatic effect.

The first twelve lines have a sustained, melodious rhythm as they move towards the end of the sentence on line 12, where 'you can't breathe'. At this point the earth replies, as the third stanza changes into clear short **statements**: 'No, they whisper. You own nothing.' The final three lines are self-contained, abrupt and admonishing, reminders that a human being's visiting 'moment' on earth is short and not open to negotiation.

Language

The use of the **list** on line 4 has the effect of sounding like part of a public speech. As the size of the area 'owned' expands, the pride in one's achievement increases.

Alliteration and **consonance** are used effectively in the second stanza. The gentle sustained 's' and 'r' sounds as the 'trees unloose/their soft arms around you' suits the quiet withdrawal of support; 'the birds take back their language' uses repetition of a more forceful 'b' ; 'the cliffs fissure and collapse', with the cracking harsh letter 'c'. Can you recognise a tone of disapproval in the **repetition** of the plosive 'p' on line 15: '*planting the flag, proclaiming*'?

Note the repetition also of the pronoun 'you' in the final stanza — almost as though the finger is being pointed and the word accompanied by prodding. The natural planet may 'whisper' but its message is strong and convincing.

> **Pause for thought**
>
> Why do you think Atwood uses direct speech? Is this an effective way of giving the earth a voice?

Imagery

The first stanza can be read literally or the 'long voyage' understood as a **metaphor** for human life. Perhaps the 'centre of your room' is implying the reaching of a final state of important achievement, at which point the universe revolves around you and you feel you can play God.

And what happens if human beings play God with the planet? The second stanza describes how, without responsible and respectful earth management, the earth will die. Key aspects of the natural world are **personified** as though the earth suffers a heart attack: the trees can no longer sustain life and so remove their support; the birds stop singing and speech disappears; the cliffs 'collapse'; and life is extinct.

> **Grade *booster***
>
> Analyse the simile on line 11 to raise your marks. Think about the way a wave pulls back and leaves you stranded. Oxygen levels in the atmosphere continue to fall due to human activities such as burning fossil fuels and deforestation, and living organisms — including humans — will suffocate without sufficient oxygen.

Ideas to consider

This poem would probably be very effective if read aloud like a procla-mation. It uses oratorical techniques: a forceful list, direct speech and a pattern of three strong statements at the end.

Is it 'the moment when…' we 'say, *I own this*' that destroys our relation-ship with nature? Does the act of control destroy, as we push it away in attempting to pervert it? Atwood may be suggesting that humanity's urge to control is unnatural — an act of destruction — and the more control we seek to exert, the wider and deeper the destruction becomes.

'Cold Knap Lake' by Gillian Clarke

Context

Gillian Clarke was born in Cardiff, Wales, in 1937. She still lives in west Wales on a smallholding where she and her husband have a small flock of sheep. She is a tutor of creative writing and enjoys working with children and adults. A Welsh and English speaker, she has travelled in Europe and the USA giving readings of her poetry, which is studied throughout the UK at GCSE and A-level.

Although many of her poems, like 'Cold Knap Lake' and 'Neighbours', are based on personal experience, she uses her close affinity with the natural world and her native Wales to explore wider issues and themes. Her website: www.gillianclarke.co.uk/home.htm offers a lot of interesting information.

What happens?

The poet recalls an incident that happened when she was young. A child, presumed drowned, was pulled out of the lake. Watched by an awed crowd, the poet's mother administered the kiss of life to the little girl and managed to resuscitate her. When Clarke's father took the little girl home to her parents she was 'thrashed for almost drowning'.

Reflecting on the memory as an adult, the poet wonders whether she really witnessed the event in such detail or whether her imagination has embellished the reality, due to other people's narratives or even her love of fairy stories, nursery rhymes and folk tales that she enjoyed as a six-year-old child. Although she was very proud of her mother, she feels that in her child's inventive mind there were more sinister, threatening aspects to the child's close escape, and time, with its 'shadowy' recollections, is unable to make anything clearer.

Structure

The poem is written in alternating four and six line stanzas with a separate **rhyming couplet** at the end. 'Water' and 'daughter' are **full rhymes**, to stress their importance, bring the poem to a clear conclusion and perhaps suggest that 'all lost things...under closing water' are now likely to remain 'lost'. Note also the rhyming 'there' and 'air', which enclose the vague 'troubled' and fanciful questioning of stanza four.

Elsewhere Clarke uses **half rhyme** to gently connect the lines in each stanza: earth/breath; bowed/soaked; silent/it, and also **internal rhyme**: bowed/crowd; red head/dread — all examples in stanza two.

Language and imagery

Written as a **first-person narrative**, it is not clear who 'We' refers to, but gradually the drama unfolds and we realise that the poet is describing an incident that happened around the time of the Second World War, when she was a young child with her parents.

Alliteration is used to heighten the drama when the crowd is 'drawn by the dread of it' (l. 10) and stanza four has a mysterious, almost whispered, tone with its sibilant 's' sounds and repeated **onomatopoeic** letter 'w' in 'heavy webs of swans/as their wings beat and whistle on the air'.

The incident is remembered in full **colour**: a 'blue-lipped' supposedly drowned child, 'green silk' water, the 'red head' of the mother and the adjective 'rosy' to describe the recovering child.

The poet's pride in her mother's life-saving actions is obvious. Her mother is 'a heroine' who reverently kneels 'on the earth…her red head bowed' as though in prayer. The giving of 'her breath' to 'a stranger's child' sounds selfless and more generous than simply the act of mouth-to-mouth resuscitation. Could the revived child's 'bleating' be associated with the resurrected Christ or Lamb of God?

The **tone** of the poem changes for stanza four, and lines 16–20 (no longer narrative) are all one long sentence. The poet questions whether 'something else shadowy' was under the surface of the lake, but she cannot come up with answers for her confused drawn-out wonderings.

An effective use of **personification** is the description of 'the dipped fingers of willows'. Usually, graceful willow trees would conjure up a peaceful setting but the imagined image of them pushing down into 'the troubled surface' is threatening. The smooth 'satiny mud' rises to 'bloom' on the surface of the water, but it creates 'cloudiness' not beauty, when swans, for once depicted as 'heavy' rather than elegant, disturb the edge of the lake.

Ideas to consider

The 'poor man's daughter' lives in a 'poor house' and the use of 'poor' sets the poem in its 1939–45 period, when the differences between the social classes would be obvious to a child from a wealthier family. Witnessing a child being 'thrashed for almost drowning' would seem shocking to the poet's father, as it does to his daughter and the readers of her poem. The explanation, however, is not connected to poverty, rather an old-fashioned

> **Pause for thought**
>
> The mother's everyday 'wartime cotton frock' contrasts with the exotic texture of the 'water's long green silk' in which the 'drowned child' is 'dressed'. Do you think the child seems to be wearing a fairytale gown in the poet's memory? Is she thinking of Millais' painting of Ophelia? Why does the narrator seem rather unmoved by the sight of a child who 'lay for dead'?

> **Grade *booster***
>
> Examine the effect of the sudden, short question 'Was I there?' on line 15. The poet seems to remember the event clearly but then turns the poem around with three short words to concentrate on the dividing line between memory and truth.

punishment given out of relief that the child is safe and as an apology for any 'fuss' that she might have caused.

Gillian Clarke explains on her website: 'When you recapture a memory from early childhood, you're sometimes not sure if you were really there, if someone told you about it, or if you read it in a story.' Is this true of your very early recollections?

'Price we pay for the sun' by Grace Nichols

Context

Grace Nichols was born in a small coastal village in Guyana in 1950. When she was eight years old she moved with her family to Georgetown, the capital of Guyana, where she experienced her country's fight for independence from the UK, eventually gained in 1966. She worked as a teacher and journalist, which nurtured an interest in the folk stories and traditions of Guyana. When she was 27, she emigrated with her daughter and her partner, the poet John Agard, to the UK, where she still lives.

Nichols enjoys exploring cultural differences in the subjects and language of her poems, writing in Standard English and Guyanese Creole (the language resulting from a mixture of other languages).

PHB.cz/Fotolia

What happens?

Nichols explores the differences in the way people perceive the Caribbean. While tourists view the islands as being idyllic with their sea, sand and palm trees, the reality is that the native people live in poverty. 'Price we pay for the sun' also suggests exploitation of these 'picture postcard' islands. While the comparatively wealthy can afford their Caribbean holiday, the indigenous West Indians 'pay' daily by their hard lifestyle in tropical weather conditions.

Structure

The poem is written in three separate free-verse stanzas, the last three-lined stanza standing apart from the rest of the poem to speak the message of the poem directly to the reader.

The rhythm of the poem seems to place emphasis on the final word of most lines, but on lines 10 and 16, each followed by a single-word line, the main stress is held back to lay the stress on the lone word: 'these islands split/**bone**'; 'cancer tricking her/**below**'.

Extra emphasis is also given to 'below' (l. 17) by **rhyming** it with 'know' (l. 14); in a similar way 'bone' (l. 11) and 'stone' (l. 8) are full rhymes, ending the first stanza dramatically. In the final lines, the internal rhyme 'sun' with 'run come' pulls the three words together.

Language

Nichols uses **repetition** in the first stanza to emphasise her point. '**These islands**' are proclaimed three times: they are not idyllic tourist locations; they are '**real**/more **real**/than flesh and blood'; '**past** stone/**past** foam' — there is far more to them than can be seen.

'Poverty is the price we pay for the sun' uses the plosive **alliterative** 'p' to create a forceful end statement, full of conviction. The same letter can give a tone of distaste to 'picture postcards' and stress the importance of the repeated word 'past'. The 'w' sounds on lines 18 and 19 build up the sound of the wind (notice the onomatopoeic 'whipping') before the 'hurricanes' on the following line. 'Sifting sand' reproduces the constant susurration of shaken sand while reminding us of the grandmother moaning softly for her sick daughter.

> *Key quotation*
>
> **Poverty is the price we pay for the sun**

Imagery

The poet's sparing and minimalist vocabulary allows for a great deal of **ambiguity**. The poet's biological mother could also represent the country of her birth, her mother country; her father could also suggest the land of her forefathers. While describing her family's suffering and anguish due to her mother's

> **Pause for thought**
>
> The metaphor 'these islands split bone' suggests many ideas: they will destroy you; they are dry to the core; they last longer and are deeper than flesh and blood; they demand hard work and gruelling poverty to survive. Can you explain what the words mean to you?

breast cancer, the extreme conditions of a tropical climate and mountainous landscape are detailed:

- The simile 'my mother's breasts like sleeping volcanoes' carries the full connotation of a disease ready to erupt. The cancer is 'tricking' her like a fire 'below'. Volcanoes are caused by processes beneath the surface of the earth and islanders can only wait in fear for an eruption when sulphur dioxide gas will explode from the volcano. In such a way Nichols' family can only wait, angry ('sulph-furious') that their mother can have such a corrosive illness. Their poverty ('the price we pay') prevents them having the means to seek treatment for the mother's condition.

- The father's tears are compared metaphorically to 'salty hurricanes' as the high winds of his anguish increase and he sobs out his tears in noisy, uncontrollable pain.

- The grandmother is quieter — she sings softly, 'shushing' with the gentle reassurance of 'sifting sand'.

Ideas to consider

The last line 'run come' can seem confusing, but it is open to your interpretation. In the Creole dialect it probably means 'ran', giving one interpretation that the poet is telling the reader to 'run away' from such poverty. Was Nichols the 'girl' who ran from Guyana? Is the reader addressed as 'girl' or is the poet talking to herself? An interesting idea is that of running away but always coming back — in the same way that Nichols continues to celebrate Creole forms of language, mixing them with Standard English, so a West Indian's sense of identity could sometimes draw him or her back to their island.

The following paragraph is taken from the Guyana Tourism Authority website:

> Guyana has an irresistible combination of fascinating and breathtaking natural beauty; pristine Amazonian rain-forests, immense waterfalls, amazing wildlife, a vibrant indigenous culture, rich cultural heritage — a paradise for nature lovers, adventure seekers and the Eco tourist alike.

Having read 'Price we pay for the sun', would you feel differently about going on holiday to the Caribbean?

'Neighbours' by Gillian Clarke

Context

For information about Gillian Clarke, see 'Cold Knap Lake' on p. 58.

The Chernobyl nuclear disaster in the Ukraine on 26 April 1986 was the worst disaster in the history of nuclear power. Thirty-one people were killed immediately and about 600,000 workers (mainly volunteers) who took part in recovery and clean-up operations were exposed to high levels of radiation when radioactive elements, including xenon gas, iodine and caesium, exploded into the atmosphere. Much of the fallout was deposited close to Chernobyl and 350,000 people moved out of the area and settled elsewhere. Wind direction and heavy rainfall, carrying radioactive fallout, also affected many countries in the northern hemisphere, some areas (such as Scandinavia) worse than others.

Caesium contamination will remain in the soil for many years. As a result of the disaster, 9,700 farms and more than four million sheep were under restriction across the UK. About 4,000 children and young adults who drank milk contaminated with iodine have since been treated (successfully in most cases) for thyroid cancer.

You can watch a video clip of Clarke talking about this poem on the BBC Learning Zone website. She explains that she wanted to show how a disaster like Chernobyl connects everyone across the world:

> I wanted to show how enraged and upset and hurt everyone must be about an accident like that happening and no warning, no warning, nothing to say...I was full of heartbreak and rage and despair, followed by hope.

Glossary

isobars (l. 2) lines drawn on a weather map connecting places that have the same atmospheric pressure: lines close together indicate a strong pressure gradient, creating conditions for strong winds

migrating (l. 6) travelling from one region to another at certain times of the year

fjords (l. 7) long, narrow, deep inlets of the sea between steep slopes

gall (l. 7) bitter fluid

caesium (l. 13) radioisotope caesium-137, with a half-life of 30.2 years

democracy (l. 19) a political system where citizens elect their government

virus (l. 19) type of germ that causes disease; a poisoning influence

toxin (l. 19) a poisonous substance

Glasnost (l. 22) a policy of the former Soviet Union, to be more open and honest with discussion of social problems and shortcomings

Golau glas (l. 22) light sky; blue light

What happens?

Describing the impact of the Chernobyl disaster, Clarke writes from her personal viewpoint. Fearful of what would arrive with high winds, the fears of the Welsh were justified when the natural seasonal behaviour of animals was affected. Many birds never survived migration, due to effects of radioactive fallout, and national news reported the widespread poisonous effects on other countries. Despite the passage of time there were still deposits of caesium in the Welsh peat and iodine in the rain.

Something positive, however, may have resulted from the disaster: countries across the world are starting to talk together and perhaps be more tolerant of each 'neighbour's' politics — surely a hopeful sign.

Grade *booster*

Analyse the effectiveness of 'blowback' to improve your response. Not only does it suggest the violent effect of nuclear reaction, but also hints at secret intelligence services between the East and the West. On a simpler level it links to the dangerous wind blowing from the Ukraine with its 'bitter air'.

Structure

Seven three-lined stanzas of free verse are followed by a stand-alone line. This **separated** line, with its two clear caesuras, is divided into three, bringing together three languages: Russian, Welsh and English in the spirit of neighbourliness.

The **enjambement** between lines 9 and 10 cuts across stanzas, emphasising 'the blowback', with its forceful multilayered connotation.

Language

There is a recurring **theme** of betrayed innocence in the first five stanzas:

- The lamb (l. 3), usually a symbol of innocence, spring and new life, has not survived and the reader is shocked by a scavenging bird drinking from its eye. On line 13 a live lamb is still under threat from deposits of caesium on the land.
- Finland is a large, flat and cold country and it is very poignant that 'small birds' fall there.
- Small, sweet-singing song-thrushes, warblers and nightingales all have their songs hushed as their 'wing-beats fail'. Children have to be warned that the little birds they have grown to care about are 'dangerous'.
- 'A child, lifting her head to drink the rain' is unaware that iodine has the potential to give her thyroid cancer.

Pause for thought

The word 'neighbour' can mean your fellow human being as well as somebody who is situated near you or lives close by. Can you recognise how Clarke is suggesting that countries should be more truthful to one another? She is using her voice in the poem to express her political opinion.

The **tone** of the vocabulary changes on line 19, when fear, anger and despair change to hope with words such as 'twinned', 'each heart', 'democracy', 'green in its voice', 'break of blue'. Countries that seemed to have little in common are now, since the disaster, beginning to 'talk' in a more open and 'neighbourly' way. No country or state can live in isolation when such dangers can be carried across borders by wind and rain.

The 's' sound is used particularly effectively in stanza two, where the birdsong can be heard in the words. Their 'small' deaths are therefore all the more distressing. On line 13 the gentle lamb 'sips caesium' and the **alliterative** 's' sounds sinister and deadly. The last line purposefully repeats the harsh letter 'g' alongside sibilant 's' sounds, followed by a plosive, but gentler, repeated 'b', which imparts a wishful tone to the final phrase.

Imagery

Clarke uses **metaphors** to express alternative interpretations:

- 'shouldering isobars' (l. 2) suggests the lines predicting the toxic winds are close together, while inferring that the distance between other countries and the Ukraine is small — too close for comfort. To 'shoulder' can also mean to carry a heavy burden, as the wind carries dangerous radioactive materials.
- 'smudged signatures on light' gives a sad picture of small dark birds falling from the sky, their lungs poisoned — perhaps their feeble struggles suggest the scribble of a hasty signature in dark ink on white paper.
- The 'box of sorrows' (l. 12) is probably a reference to Pandora's Box in the Greek myth, which, when opened, let out all the evils of the world. Only Hope remained at the end, just as Clarke's optimism hopes for 'a first break of blue' at the end of the poem.
- 'the poisoned arrow' suggests the child is harmed rather than killed immediately by her small action of swallowing the slanting rain. An arrow has to be shot — so who is to blame?
- 'green in its voice' gives healthy song back to the migrating bird and hopes that, owing to this dreadful accident, countries can produce energy that is guaranteed safer for the global environment.

> *Key quotation*
>
> **In the democracy of the virus and the toxin**
>
> **we wait.**

Ideas to consider

Do you feel the poet is more concerned about the birds and lambs than the firemen who lost their lives in the disaster and 'the child on the Moscow train' (probably a photo selected by the media after the disaster)? How does she show that the disaster caused international distress?

Pick out lines that imply consequences to whole eco-structures.

'Crossing the loch' by Kathleen Jamie

Context

Born in Renfrewshire in 1962, Kathleen Jamie is one of Scotland's leading contemporary poets. She studied philosophy at Edinburgh University, has written eight collections of poetry and presently lectures in Creative Writing at St Andrew's University. She lives in Fife.

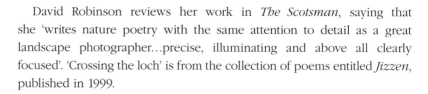

David Robinson reviews her work in *The Scotsman*, saying that she 'writes nature poetry with the same attention to detail as a great landscape photographer…precise, illuminating and above all clearly focused'. 'Crossing the loch' is from the collection of poems entitled *Jizzen*, published in 1999.

Glossary

sickle-shaped (l. 2) in the shape of a crescent

race (l. 11) a strong or swift current of water.

deadheads (l. 14) partially-submerged logs, floating nearly vertically

hulls (l. 14) the outer casings of rockets, guided missiles or submarines

phosphorescence (l. 19) seen at night when the water is disturbed, largely due to organisms like plankton, which give out brief brightly-coloured light

bow wave (l. 23) the wave that forms at the front of a boat when it moves through the water

foolhardy (l. 24) rash, reckless, not thinking about the danger

blaeberries (l. 29) wild blueberries, bilberries

What happens?

The poet recalls how one night she and some friends left the bright cordial atmosphere of the pub and pushed a rowing boat out on an open loch. Rowing away from the shore and into rougher waters, their jokiness subsides as they grow fearful. It is growing cold and the deep dark water could contain dangerous obstacles. She cannot remember specific details but recollects their joint apprehension, when suddenly marine phosphorescence lights up the boat and its 'astonished' occupants.

Looking back on the incident years later, Jamie admits it was a risky thing to have done, but recognises the impetuosity and self-assurance of youth that gave them such a magical experience.

> **Key quotation**
>
> calling our own
>
> the sky and
> salt-water

Structure

The autobiographical account begins with 'Remember', a common introduction to a recalled incident. Using frequent **enjambement** and **caesura** to suggest natural speech, the poem is written in four stand-alone stanzas of free verse: the first two seven-lined stanzas introduce the situation; the third nine-lined stanza describes the highlight of the memory; the final (also nine-lined) stanza reflects on the experience at a later date.

Jamie does not use rhyme but brings the final lines of the poem to an obvious conclusion by the use of **assonance**:

...the glimmering anklets

we w**or**e in the shallows

as we shipped **oar**s and jumped,

to dr**aw** the boat safe, high at the cottage sh**ore**.

The repeated long, round 'or' sound, gives a feeling of homecoming and safety as the boat is pulled up on dry land.

Language and imagery

Jamie's poetry has a musical feel to it and she chooses long sustained letters such as 'r' and 'l' to create an emotive watery atmosphere. Look at the alliterative 'l' in lines 9 and 10: 'and the spi**ll**/of the **l**och reached **l**ong into the night'. An increased number of words with the letter 'w' are used on lines 19–21, including the sound image 'twittering'. Perhaps the letter suggests the wonder and amazement felt as the bright sparkles light up 'fingers and oars'.

> **Pause for thought** ❙❙
>
> Compare 'the hunched hills' (l. 19) to the next line's 'ticking nuclear hulls'. The hills around the loch may seem threatening, but the sudden mention of a nuclear missile in the water, by changing 'i' to 'u' creates a sinister mood for the spirited young people who previously had given no thought to the loch's potential dangers.

Lines 6 and 7 rely on 'l' again, using **onomatopoeia** with the words 'lipped' and 'boat', to put across the sounds of the waves lapping at the side of the boat and the small deep echoes made by enclosed water. 'The oars' splash, creak' are the only sounds to be heard when laughter is 'hushed' on the dark loch.

The feelings experienced that evening are remembered acutely but the details as to what individuals did or said are not — this is emphasised by the **repetition** of the word 'who' (ll. 15, 16). 'The cottage', small and homely after a big adventure, is also repeated at the end of the poem to show journey's end has been safely reached.

The first and last stanzas are each one long sentence as the memory is reflected upon. Line 8 is in sharp contrast, with two short statements to describe the start of the journey, when the rowing begins and the talking suddenly stops.

The poem is rich in **imagery**:
- with many **metaphors** — 'the spill of the loch', 'the cold shawl of breeze', 'hunched hills', 'salt-air and stars', 'hauled', 'deep into lungs', 'small boat of saints', 'the magic dart of our bow wave', 'dark-starred by blaeberries', 'glimmering anklets'
- examples of effective **personification** — 'after the pub loosed us through its swinging doors',

> **Grade *booster*** !
>
> Do not try to write about all the effective images. Select one or two and analyse them in detail, e.g. 'the magic dart of our bow wave' suggests the water, pushed into an arrow shape from the front of the boat, is glistening in a mysterious and enchanting way.

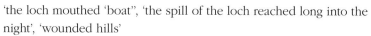

'the loch mouthed 'boat'', 'the spill of the loch reached long into the night', 'wounded hills'

- and two **similes** — 'as though the loch mouthed 'boat'', 'like a twittering nest washed from the rushes'

Ideas to consider

Jamie describes the illuminated boat and its excited occupants as 'a twittering nest/washed from the rushes, an astonished/small boat of saints'. Saints are usually depicted with golden haloes or lit up like angels. Here there is perhaps a link also to the story of Moses hidden in the basket in the bulrushes. The 'twittering nest' suggests not only the innocence of fledglings afloat, but also the coracle that brought saints like Saint Columba with his followers to Iona, a Scottish island.

'Calling our own/the sky and salt water' is an interesting reflection on the confidence of youth. Do you think young people are more reckless with outdoor pursuits because of their enthusiasm for new adventures or are they 'foolhardy' because of peer group pressure?

'Hard water' by Jean Sprackland

Context

Jean Sprackland (born 1962) was brought up in the Staffordshire brewing town of Burton-on-Trent. The poet says she 'came to see the water as embodying a whole lot of things about that town, and about growing up: hardness, frankness (of the 'calling a spade a spade' variety) and sourness, but also at the same time slipperiness, change, complication and ambivalence'.

She studied English and philosophy at university, began to write poetry when she was 30 and now has three collections of published poetry. She presently lives in Southport, Merseyside.

What happens?

Sprackland celebrates the qualities of the hard water she grew up with in the Midlands. She describes the 'anaesthetic' water from the tap and the heavy uncompromising rain, while comparing the water to the characteristics of Staffordshire people who, with plain-spoken acceptance of their lifestyle, believe in working hard to make an honest living. Those who grew up in this place, she concludes, retain a strong sense of their identity for the rest of their lives.

Structure

Written in three free-verse stanzas of unequal length, the first three lines describe the poet's experience of 'soft' water when she was 'on holiday in Wales'. The first word 'but' of stanza two shifts her allegiances quickly to detailed descriptions of the hard Midlands water. The third stanza begins with Sprackland's personal experiences when walking home on rainy nights, before moving on to her final reflections.

The technique of **caesura** is used particularly effectively on lines 5, 17 and 18. 'Flat. Straight.' presents the two single adjectives alone without further embellishment, in the way the Midlands accent pronounces vowels. The short statement 'It couldn't lie.' is short and direct. 'No salt —' gives a sense of the poet's thoughts following through, as though speaking directly to the reader. Salt enhances the flavour of food — Sprackland wants 'the true taste' (l. 23).

Pause for thought

Lines 10–13 do not contain a verb. How effective is this economy of language?

Language

The poem is written in the first person, giving a personal viewpoint in a **conversational style**. The use of colloquial **dialogue** on lines 6 and 25 gives clear examples of dialect to support the 'straight talk'.

The **alliterative** 'soft stuff' on line 1 with its instant dismissive tone announces the poet's opinion that water from elsewhere is inferior — too flippant in the way it results in 'excitable soap'. The 'sour steam' emerging from the cooling towers, however, is reliable and practical.

The **repetition** of the word 'taste' on lines 23 and 24 emphasises the many connotations of the word: to distinguish flavours in the mouth; a personal preference or liking; the ability to discern what is excellent; the sense of what is proper; to experience or appreciate something. The poet likes the taste of 'work', 'the true taste of early mornings' and 'the blunt taste' of a temperament that wants no fuss and uses its 'cleverness' in day-to-day living. Only after these tastings is the water described as 'lovely'.

The poem relies on many **adjectives** describing the water, to **symbolise** how Sprackland feels about her home town and her sense of 'belonging' — 'straight', 'honest', 'clean', 'fierce' etc.

Key quotation

...the blunt taste of *don't get mardy,* of *too bloody deep for me,*

Grade *booster*

This is a sensuous poem. Improve your mark by explaining, with apt quotation, how the senses of taste, touch and smell complement each other to give the reader a physical experience of water.

Imagery

The poet uses a great deal of **personification** in her poem. Water straight from the tap has 'a fizz of anxiety'. Unlike the emotional, frivolous 'soft stuff', Midlands water is given the human quality of honesty, and limestone that of 'frankness'. In this way she links her feelings about the water to her perceptions of the people who live and work in this area. On cold, wet nights the 'pitiless' weather conditions are severe and cruel, the driving rain burning her face. Burton-on-Trent is so far from the coast that the rain there has 'forgotten the sea'.

'Like the vowels, like the straight-talk', the 'flat' water is compared to the short, blunt way of speaking.

Ideas to consider

Drinking water in most areas of England is considered to be very hard. Areas with softer water are Wales, parts of the north-west, Devon and Cornwall. Water is deliberately hardened with gypsum by the brewing industry to bring out the flavour of the hops. This process is called Burtonisation, from Burton-on-Trent, a town famous for brewing beer because of the chemicals in the water. Beer, says Sprackland, has 'its own repertoire of contradictions and its own capacity to change people'.

One of Burton's well-known landmarks until 2006 was the Drakelow Power Station, with its cooling towers that have now been demolished.

Have you noticed the differences in the water when you travel around the country? People accustomed to hard water are surprised by the amount of soap suds produced in soft water areas and those used to soft water find lots more detergent is required in the washing machine. Some people claim that water tasting of minerals does not make good tea — the poet's initial surprise by the change in water is expressed in the words: 'a mania of teadrinking and hairwashing'.

Poems from the English literary heritage

'London' by William Blake

Context

William Blake (1757–1827) was an English poet, illustrator, printmaker and visionary mystic who expressed his political, social and philosophical ideas through the works he created. He was born in Soho, London, where he spent most of his life. Although a religious man, in his poetry he criticised the role in society of the Church of England. Viewed by many as an eccentric outsider, he sympathised with the actions of French revolutionaries who, at the time this poem was written, were rising up against the monarchy and the Church in Paris.

Glossary

chartered (l. 1) owned, rented or licensed for business purposes

woe (l. 4) intense grief or misery

manacles (l. 8) handcuffs

appalls (l. 10) fills with horror or alarm that causes one to become pale

hapless (l. 11) deserving pity; unfortunate

harlot (l. 14) female prostitute

blights (l. 16) ruins

plagues (l. 16) sexually transmitted diseases

hearse (l. 16) a vehicle for carrying a coffin to a church or cemetery.

What happens?

Blake hated the effects of the Industrial Revolution in England, and in 'London' he describes the city and its people as ailing and corrupt, where industrialisation promotes poverty, child labour, disease and prostitution.

Structure

The poem is written in four four-lined stanzas (quatrains) with **alternate lines rhyming**. The metre, predominantly **iambic tetrameter**, creates a tightly structured poem with a sense of entrapment, which entirely mirrors the 'chartered' lives of its poor inhabitants. Sometimes the heavy beat falls on the first syllable of the line to place extra stress on a particular word: 'Marks' (l. 4) and 'Blasts' (l. 15), for example. The second stanza, however, never changes from its remorseless **pounding iambic metre**.

Language and imagery

To put across his tone of anger and condemnation, Blake uses **repetition**:

- The repetition of 'in every' (a technique called anaphora when at the beginning of consecutive lines, as here) is a declamation to be heard, reminding its readers of what they would rather not admit to — that the whole of society is suffering together: trapped, repressed and controlled.
- The adjective 'chartered' on lines 1 and 2 emphasises his indignation that not only is the city privately owned, but even the river, to which all people should have free access, is controlled by laws.
- The verb 'mark' (l. 2) is repeated in the next line as 'marks of weakness, marks of woe'. The poet notices on his wanderings how

scarred and damaged the poor are by those in authority who do nothing to change the laws that benefit only the wealthy.

- 'cry' suggests weeping, wailing, shouting, exclaiming, announcing, appealing and any loud vocalisation of emotions such as fear, anger and despair. It is, therefore, an effective word to use three times, when describing the sounds of this city of 'woe'. Blake's vocabulary may seem simple at times, particularly when he repeats the same word, but his purpose is to give the poem a song-like quality. This poem is from his poetry collection called *Songs of Experience*.

- 'I hear' (ll. 8, 13) reminds the reader of the aural sounds of discontent and misery.

Key quotation

In every voice, in every ban,

The mind-forged manacles I hear:

Pause for thought

The word 'ban' (l. 7) carries a wealth of restriction in only three letters. Think of the Ten Commandments: 'Thou shalt not...' with no room for negotiation. As well as a prohibition, a ban can mean a curse. Does this ambiguity add to your appreciation of stanza two?

Occasional use of **alliteration** conveys the poet's despair and accompanying anger. Note how the letters 'm' and 'b' are used. 'Marks', 'mind-forged manacles' and line 13: 'most through midnight streets' employ the long sustained 'm' sound, which can be held longer for emphasis; the plosive 'b' in 'ban', 'black'ning', 'blood', 'Blasts', 'new-born', 'blights' explodes from the lips to join the crying and cursing on the London streets.

The **metaphor** 'the mind-forged manacles' contains the main message of the poem. Londoners in Blake's time would have seen the strong, metal handcuffs and shackles on convicts heading for prison or to the ships for deportation, and would be terrified by the image. The chains endured by the people are the restrictions imposed by external authorities, which take away all aspects of freedom. 'Mind-forged' also suggests that the people are so brainwashed into seeing themselves as helpless that they do not even think of the possibility of rebelling, unlike their French counterparts at this time. The child chimney-sweep is exploited; the soldier is treated brutally; the young 'harlot's' baby is a hindrance to her mother's trade and born into poverty and disease. The prostitute passes venereal disease to men who marry only for convenience and seek out prostitutes, so continuing the cycle of misery.

Grade booster

Analyse the ironic antithesis: 'Every black'ning church appalls' (l. 10). The archaic meaning of 'appalls' is to make pale, and could also be a play on the idea of a funeral pall (a dark cloth put over a coffin, usually with a cross on it to symbolise Christ's victory over sin and death). It also suggests 'to disgust', implying that the church should be ashamed of the way it allows child chimney-sweeps to be abused by dangerous, harsh working conditions.

The **oxymoron** of 'the marriage hearse' depicts the respectable idea of marriage on its way to death by disease and deceit.

Ideas to consider

This poem could be described as a political protest. Do you find its tone to be one of complete despair? Blake is implying that change is required and he even lists the causes of the misery and wretchedness of those who are suffering. Is there hope in the way he can express his anger through his poetry or is he totally pessimistic?

Extract from 'The prelude' by William Wordsworth

JPagetRFphotos/Fotolia

Context

William Wordsworth was born in 1770 and spent most of his adult life in Grasmere and Rydal, right in the heart of the Lake District, an area he loved very much. He lived for 80 years and wrote some of England's greatest Romantic poetry. His autobiographical poem, 'The prelude', traces his growth from when he was a boy until the time it was written and he seems to have developed his identity and inspiration from the landscape around him. Orphaned at 13, he spent a great deal of time outdoors and alone with nature for company, which in turn fed his lively imagination.

What happens?

Wordsworth describes an incident when, as a child, he stole a small boat 'one summer evening' and rowed it confidently

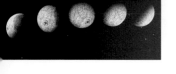

up the lake towards what he thought was a ridge on the horizon. Suddenly a huge menacing peak reared up behind the ridge and appeared to stride towards him 'like a living thing'. Terrified, he turned back, moored the boat and returned home in a 'grave and serious mood'. For a long time he was haunted by the experience, the familiar world of nature seeming unreal and threatening in his child's imagination.

Structure

The extract is written in one continuous stanza of free verse. The slow and calm **iambic pentameter** is ideal for the descriptive and thoughtful narrative. Frequent **enjambement** also adds a sense of storytelling — you can almost feel the gentle rowing movement at times.

Language

Notice how the **tone** of the poem changes. It is with mischievous excitement that the boy steals the boat — with 'troubled pleasure', and appreciates the beauty of the moonlight on the water: 'Small circles glittering idly…Until they melted all into one track/Of sparkling light'. With confidence and vigour he rows 'lustily' until line 21. As the 'huge peak' rises menacingly, fear causes the boy to turn the boat 'with trembling oars' to return 'in grave and serious mood'. The extract finishes with a depressing 'darkness'.

Wordsworth does not run out of words to use when he **repeats** the adjective 'huge' on line 22. Instead he concentrates, as a child would, on stressing the vastness of the black peak that appears so suddenly. It is also interesting that his 'troubled pleasure' is part of his excitement at the start of the adventure, yet on the last line the remembered 'spectacle' has become 'a trouble to my dreams' — a persistent nightmare. 'Still' (ll. 25, 26) reinforces the menace that continues, to an increasing degree, to pursue its terrified prey.

The dominant image of the poem is the **personified** black peak. Wordsworth describes how it 'upreared its head…with purpose of its own…and…strode after [him]'. The **simile** comparing the looming mountain to 'a living thing' depicts the way the imagination plays tricks on the mind of an unsuspecting and impressionable child. He cannot make sense of how the familiar world of nature could take on such a disturbing character.

The account begins with the words 'One summer evening…' and goes on to describe an idyllic setting and Wordsworth's world of nature. He is 'led by her' (nature) in his appreciation of his beloved Lake District, its beauty and its solitude. The simple line 'I dipped my oars into the silent lake' holds the placid sound of night-time rowing and is in contrast to the later lines where 'huge and mighty forms' disturb his relationship with the natural world.

Ideas to consider

Do you think the young boy sees the incident as a punishment for taking the boat on the lake without permission? Wordsworth is one of the British Romantic poets who placed an emphasis on the emotions of childhood to understand the world. They also explored the relationship between nature and human life in their poetry, considering personal experiences and the power of the imagination to be important.

Re-read line 20. Do you think a swan 'heaves' through the water? Is this an effective simile?

'The wild swans at Coole' by W. B. Yeats

Context

William Butler Yeats (1865–1939) was an Irish poet and dramatist. Born in Dublin, educated in Dublin and England, he spent much of his childhood in County Sligo with his maternal grandparents. 'The wild swans at Coole' was written in 1917, a critical period in Yeats's adult life. He had seen the outbreak of the First World War as well as the 1916 Easter Rising in Ireland and in his personal life he had suffered repeated rejections of his marriage proposals to Maud Gonne and her daughter. Coole Park, in County Galway, the estate of his friend and patron Lady Augusta Gregory, was close to his own summer home and he retreated there to draw inspiration from its beauty.

Glossary

clamorous (l. 12)
insistently noisy

companionable (l. 21)
friendly; sociable

attend upon (l. 24)
accompany

What happens?

Yeats, himself in the autumn of life, describes the lovely and familiar spectacle of many wild swans on Coole Park lake in October. He reflects, in melancholy mood, that in the 19 years since he first visited the park, there have been many changes in his life and the world around him. Yet the swans, still full of vigour and passion, remain untouched by the passing of time. The 'mysterious, beautiful' swans seem immortal, in contrast to his own advancing age.

Structure

The poem consists of five six-lined stanzas, each with an underlying **iambic metre**. Sometimes the iambic rhythm is strong and regular, as in the poignant line:

> And **now**/my **heart**/is **sore**

Elsewhere the first syllable of the line is stressed to place emphasis on a particular word — see lines 3, 4, 10, 15, 18, 23. Line 22 demands this reversal in order to compare the way the swans seem to remain young when his heart has 'grown old'.

Yeats once jokingly told his audience: 'It gave me a devil of a lot of trouble to get into verse the poems that I am going to read and that is why I will not read them as if they were prose!' It is important, therefore, that you read this poem aloud and hear the musical rhythm. Yeats's poems have such lyrical qualities that several have been put to music by contemporary Irish recording artists.

There are frequent examples of **enjambement** that contribute to this lyricism by requiring a slight pause, before dropping to the next line. Read lines 3 and 4 to understand how this works.

There is a reflective mood to the pattern of long and short lines repeated in each stanza. The **rhyme scheme** is also consistently abcbdd, with occasional near rhymes.

Language and imagery

Yeats sets the poem in October, when 'the trees are in their autumn beauty' and **symbolic** of the poet's own late middle age, when he sadly reflects that his own life is progressing rapidly; how he has changed since his youth; and how he will die in the not too distant future — just as the winter will soon arrive. Swans are a common symbol in poetry, often used to depict the calm beauty of nature. In this poem they are **personified**, representing an unchanging ideal: they seem immortal, forever young — 'unwearied still', with no fear of ageing. To them the cold water is 'compan-

Grade *booster*

Explain how, by delaying line 18, Yeats is able to get across his continuing affection for the swans. He could have written: 'All's changed since I trod with a lighter tread', yet he pauses to reflect on their memorable effect on him 19 years earlier, before completing the sentence.

ionable' and they are faithful to each other for life. They are filled with energy and life, and the 'passion and conquest' of a young man's future 'attend upon them still'.

We know Yeats had a keen eye for observing nature by his **description** of the swans' appearance and movements. They 'mount and scatter' by clattering their feet on the water to pick up speed, before 'wheeling in great broken rings'. Notice the **long vowel sounds** here to describe the elegant birds as they smoothly spread in the air with their vast wingspans (over two metres), and beat the air, the wind whistling noisily through their 'clamorous wings'.

'Bell-beat' **alliterates** the plosive 'b' sound to reproduce the clapping sound of wings, like that of a sail in a high wind. The repeated 'c' sounds on lines 20/21 produce a musical effect and on line 23 the 'w' sounds add a feeling of freedom and fluidity.

The first stanza gives a clear, precise picture of the scene and the use of the short 'i' sound helps with this effect. 'The water/Mirrors a still sky' is a short effective statement using three techniques: the **repeated** short 'i'; the **metaphor** depicting the dull serene water reflecting the twilight sky; and the word 'still', used three times in the poem: 'still sky' (l. 4), 'attend upon them still' (l. 24), 'still water' (l. 25). They can 'still' be lovers and yet they seem to exist outside of time in a tranquillity his 'sore' heart can no longer experience.

Ideas to consider

Think about the way the tone changes throughout the poem. The peaceful scene has melancholic images of autumn and sadness. The poet envies the sight future observers will have of the swans, while presently admiring their beauty and mystery. He regrets the passing of time when 'all's changed' for him and wistfully acknowledges that they will fly away.

The tight form and iambic metre are perfect for the idea that all life has a natural cycle: that the seasons come and go; the swans migrate south each year from the Arctic tundra, but return each February; humans are born and eventually die.

If 'brilliant' (l. 13) does not mean 'intelligent' or 'superb', what other connotation could it have?

'Spellbound' by Emily Jane Brontë

Context

Emily Brontë (1818–48) lived an isolated life at the parsonage in Haworth, next to the bleak Yorkshire moors. She grew up playing imaginary games

> ### Pause for thought
>
> The heart can represent many ideas: the centre of one's deepest and sincerest feelings; one's mood; one's capacity to sympathise or be generous; courage; and, of course, love and affection. Why do you think Yeats writes: 'Their hearts have not grown old'? What could have happened to him over 19 years?

> ### Key quotation
>
> **I have looked upon those brilliant creatures,**
>
> **And now my heart is sore.**

with her sisters and brother and writing tiny books, containing stories, plays and poetry from the perspective of inhabitants of imaginative worlds. Brontë's fantasy world, Gondal, situated in the Pacific Ocean, was exotic, poetic and full of the dramatic and romantic exploits of strong-minded characters who suffered danger, imprisonment and spiritual despair. The speaker of 'Spellbound', written when Brontë was 19, is Augusta Geraldine Almeda (AGA), the fatal fictitious 'Gondal' heroine.

In 1945, Brontë stopped writing poetry and wrote her famous novel, *Wuthering Heights*, with its wild moorland setting, full of passion and beauty. She died of tuberculosis at the age of 30.

What happens?

As night approaches and the weather conditions deteriorate, a menacing storm is gathering over the high snowy landscape. Yet the speaker is unable to move. Some supernatural force seems to be constraining her and she must stay and yield to the wild elements.

Structure

The poem is written in three quatrains (four-lined stanzas), each a sentence long, with a strong **iambic metre**. The metre is reversed at the start of lines 9 and 10 to place dramatic emphasis on 'Clouds' and 'Wastes'.

Most lines are end-stopped with a strong **abab rhyme scheme** throughout. The perfect one-syllable rhymes of each second and fourth line are strengthened by the **feminine rhymes** of the first and third lines: 'round me' 'bound me'; 'bending' 'descending'; 'above me' 'move me'.

After descriptions of a huge, wild landscape in the first three lines of each song-like stanza, the last line uses short, simple words with a staccato beat. Each final line is a variation on 'I cannot go' — like a chorus (or **refrain**), giving a sense of finality as it closes with a full stop.

Language

Each stanza follows a **pattern**, starting with a dramatic description before turning to argue that escape is impossible, with the conjunctions 'But', 'And yet' and 'But' again to express the speaker's dilemma. The final line, however, demonstrates conscious submission with the words 'I will not'. The sense of paralysis described on line 3 has now become an emotional force demanding submission.

The poem uses **alliteration** to give a sense of exposure to the elements with its bleak 'bare boughs' and whistling 'wild winds'. Equally effective is the use of **assonance**. The long 'o' of 'coldly blow' may be obvious, but less so is the long 'i' sound near the start of each of the first five lines: 'n**i**ght', 'w**i**ld', 't**y**rant', '**I**', 'g**i**ant', which echoes the persistence of the escalating danger.

Brontë writes: 'I cannot, cannot go' (l. 4). Note how the **repetition** of 'cannot' stresses how sure she is that she is unable to run away from the threatening elements. Also, the repeated 'beyond' (ll. 9, 10) gives the impression of isolation, with just the huge sky above and the stretching rural wilderness below her: a position of frightening vulnerability.

Pause for thought

How does the poet emphasise the bleak, heavy mood of line 6? Look closely at the vowel sounds in the words.

Ideas to consider

'Spellbound' can be understood on two levels. You can imagine the speaker caught up in an exposed place such as the Yorkshire Moors, where the merciless elements seem to hold her in a supernatural trance, or perhaps the storm is a metaphor for a situation in life that is worsening and causing great concern. This could be a romantic entanglement, a family problem, a difficult responsibility or painful decision.

Fanny Ratchford, an expert on Brontë's poetry, suggests the speaker in the poem is a desperate mother, forced to leave her child to die on top of a mountain. She cannot leave the child to die alone, 'spellbound' by her love for the unfortunate infant. Does it change your appreciation of the poem to read this?

'Below the Green Corrie' by Norman MacCaig

Context

Norman MacCaig (1910–96) was born in Edinburgh, where he studied at the university, worked as a primary school teacher and later as a lecturer in Creative Writing and English Studies. Much of his poetry is set in Assynt, a remote area in the north-west of Scotland, where MacCaig spent a great deal of his time, especially in summer. He loved the people and the mountainous wild landscape, where he would walk, climb and fish in the corrie lakes.

In his poem 'A man in Assynt' he writes:

Who possesses this landscape? —

The man who bought it or

I who am possessed by it?

He received the OBE in 1979, the Queen's Gold Medal for Poetry in 1986 and was widely appreciated as the grand old man of Scottish poetry.

What happens?

Returning down the hillside after a visit to the Green Corrie lake, the mountains surrounding the poet seem initially menacing in 'the dark light'. However, he reflects that, over the years, rather than threaten him, they have 'enriched' his life, by filling him with a physical and spiritual love for this 'marvellous' landscape.

Structure

The poem is written in three free verse stanzas: the first setting the scene in two sentences; the second composed of three strong separate one-line statements; the third beginning with the central statement of the poem and ending with the long final image.

Language

MacCaig uses frequent **repetition**:

- 'The mountains' that introduce the poem are mentioned again in each stanza, since they are the chief images.
- Line 4, using a caesura between 'full of threats' and 'full of thunders' emphasises the degree of menace felt by the encircling heights in the gloomy dusk.
- The word 'thunders' on line 4, with its suggestion of stormy anger, changes its mood on line 7. 'They filled me with mountains and thunder' sounds more positive. Perhaps he is acknowledging that the mountains have given him all he ever asked for and from their 'thunders' he has acquired energy and strength.
- Notice how 'Their leader…full of threats' (ll. 2, 4) has changed personality completely by the end of the poem.

PHILIP ALLAN LITERATURE GUIDE **FOR GCSE**

The **tone** of the poem gradually changes. Do you feel the narrator is frightened or intimidated in the first stanza? He repeats 'they' throughout stanza two, turning around the role between man and mountain to declare respect and gratitude. By stanza three these same mountains have 'enriched' the poet's life, to become 'marvellous prowlers'.

Comparing the weather to the poet's attitude is called **pathetic fallacy**. The 'dark light' and 'ugly weather' change when a 'sunshaft' breaks through the clouds and lights up the mountain. In the same way the poet's feelings seem to move through a fear of impending danger to reflection and final exhilaration.

Grade **booster**

Concentrate on the use of individual words. 'Clambered', for example, suggests vulnerability, using hands, knees and feet to scramble down; 'infusion' could suggest the mountains have become part of him, that his life has been steeped in their magnificence.

Outlaws and adventurers

- Famous bandits (sometimes called highwaymen when on horseback), are Ned Kelly, Dick Turpin and Billy the Kid. Despite being violent lawbreakers, they have become folk-heroes, often regarded by the poor as revolutionaries and fighters for justice. One of England's most famous bandits is Robin Hood and MacCaig would have known about Rob Roy, the Scottish Robin Hood.

- The traditional greetings: 'Stand and deliver' and 'Your money or your life' leave the victims little choice. They were first quoted in trial reports of outlaws and highwaymen from between the seventeenth and nineteenth centuries, who preyed on travellers, mainly in English stagecoaches.

- Western films often depict outlaws living in the wilderness of the US Western frontier in the late nineteenth century. Sombrero-wearing Mexican bandits with their bandoliers full of bullets live on in American legend.

- The noisy, boastful swordsmen (swashbucklers) of the sixteenth century have become fearless fictional romantics (e.g. The Three Musketeers, Zorro and The Scarlet Pimpernel). Johnny Depp in *The Pirates of the Caribbean* films is a popular modern swashbuckling hero.

Liam Neeson in the film *Rob Roy*.

Everett Collection/Rex Features

Imagery

MacCaig uses an **extended metaphor** to describe the mountains and the impression they make upon him. He **personifies** the mountains, comparing them to a variety of outlaws. The 'bandits' of the first stanza are more like muggers, as they 'swagger[ed] up close in the dark light'. Stanza two, however, uses language associated with highwaymen. Stanza three's 'prowlers' may seem close behind him, yet the adjective 'marvellous' expresses his delight at their proximity, recognising their huge significance in his life.

Examine the final image. 'That swashbuckling mountain' has become a wild, courageous adventurer to be admired and respected. 'A sunshaft had pierced the clouds' contains a spear metaphor where the sun breaks through to light up the top of the mountain with its 'bandolier of light'. Do you think it is at this point that MacCaig is enlightened about his love for this Scottish landscape?

Ideas to consider

Suilven was MacCaig's special mountain and you can get a sense of the wilderness he loved by watching this YouTube link: www.youtube.com/watch?v=wBM3E6g86nY&feature=related

When he was too old to climb and was asked for the name of his favourite spot on earth, MacCaig said, 'I think it has to be the loch of the Green Corrie.'

This link: www.youtube.com/watch?v=K4UVCweoafo&feature=related shows the sun piercing the clouds and forming the shape of a sword, just like MacCaig's 'sunshaft'.

'Storm in the Black Forest' by D. H. Lawrence

Context

David Herbert Lawrence, the son of a miner, was born in Eastwood near Nottingham in 1885. By teaching miners' children, Lawrence saved enough money to attend Nottingham University College. He taught for three years before giving up due to ill health and starting to write full-time. He eloped to Bavaria, Germany, in 1912, with the wife of his former university professor and they travelled widely together, marrying in 1914. He died of tuberculosis in 1930.

Many people associate Lawrence with his novel *Lady Chatterley's Lover* (1928), which caused a scandal because of its sexual content, yet he also

Pause for thought

Why do the lines become shorter at the end? Do you think it is important for 'a bandolier of light' to have a line to itself?

Glossary

flutters (l. 5) quick, irregular movements, vibrations, tremors

uncouth (l. 9) coarse, crude, lacking in good manners

subjugated (l. 12) reduced to submission, overcome, enslaved wrote many other well-known novels, short stories, travel books, plays and almost 800 poems. His best-known poems explore the close relationship between man and nature and try to give the quality of wonder to everyday existence.

The Black Forest is an area of wooded mountains and lakes in south-west Germany, where Lawrence is believed to have stayed in 1929.

What happens?

Lawrence describes the images of a dramatic storm as night approaches. He marvels at humankind's lack of control over such wilful, magnificent forces.

rmwood1/Fotolia

Structure

The poem is written in four stanzas of free verse, with lines of varying length. Lines 4 and 13 have only three syllables, isolated for dramatic effect, and line 10 is separated from the rest of the poem. Here the desperate tone longs for relief from the stifling atmosphere.

Grade *booster*

Demonstrate how Lawrence keeps the storm moving by his use of enjambement. Lines 2/3 and 7/8 are good examples to examine. The 'liquid fire' seems to balance at the end of line 2 before it 'tipples over' and, once 'spilled' (l. 7), it halts before 'tumbling wriggling' with such energy.

Language

'And the rain won't come, the rain refuses to come!' puts across the poet's frustration that the cooling rain will not fall, by the **repetition** of two synonymous statements divided by the midline **caesura**. This short pause highlights the emotional longing for rain.

Six lines begin with 'And' as the storm escalates and the repeated verb 'wriggles'/'wriggling' emphasises the prolonged twisting movements of the lightning. Lawrence's repetition of 'supposed to' ends the poem with a tone of wonder for humankind's ineffectual power over the elements. He does not seem intimidated, but recognises the indisputable power of nature. Note the use of three exclamation marks in the final four lines.

Other poetic techniques such as **alliteration**, **assonance** and **onomatopoeia** are used. The first line sets the scene with a soothing alliterative 'n' sound: 'Now it is almost night' and the sibilant sounds of 'bronzey soft sky' create a gentle backdrop for the dramatic phenomenon about to be witnessed. Line 3: 'tipples and spills down' uses the assonant short 'i' combined with the letters 'p' and 'l' to suggest quick yet fluid movement, and the hard 'c' in 'cackle' and 'uncouth' (l. 9) breaks the silent spectacle with its harsh repetition.

Imagery

Lawrence was an artist as well as a poet, and paints pictures in the imagination with his use of **colour** words. The glow of the late evening is a 'bronzey soft sky' with flickering 'gold-bronze flutters' and the contrasting lightning changes from 'pure white' to 'bright white' and 'still brighter white' as the storm intensifies. The 'flutters' are 'bent' as though a painter's brush has lightly dabbed on to the canvas.

'Jugfull after jugfull of pure white liquid fire' (l. 2) combines two **metaphors** for an image of broad lightning cascading towards earth. The 'thick upper air' introduces the sultry atmosphere before the storm breaks. The metaphors continue in stanza two. The 'liquid fire' becomes 'electric liquid', and the forked lightning an acrobatic 'snake'.

The 'heavens' are **personified**. The thunder 'cackles' in an evil, menacing way, 'uncouth' suggesting an uncivilised din, probably offensive to mortals — as though some supernatural being is gaining pleasure from unleashing such power. Even the rain is wilful, showing contempt in its refusal to defuse the highly-charged atmosphere.

Ideas to consider

In the 1920s, electricity was the exciting fuel of the future. The National Grid system was established in 1926 to supply electricity to UK households.

With this in mind, examine the list of verbs on lines 11 and 12. 'Mastered' means to have gained control; 'chained' to have gained control by restraining or confining; 'subjugated' to have gained control by defeating or reducing to submission. Can you recognise how the gradual increase in control suggests humankind's complete knowledge and power over electricity? And yet the 'Storm in the Black Forest' with its incredible dazzling display of beauty and energy humbles Lawrence, who recognises his own insignificance alongside the planet's natural forces.

'Wind' by Ted Hughes

Context

Edward (Ted) James Hughes (1930–98) was born in Mytholmroyd, in the Calder Valley, West Yorkshire, a landscape that captured his imagination throughout his life. He wrote his first poems when he was 15 and won a scholarship to Pembroke College, Cambridge, in 1948, to study English. He was appointed England's Poet Laureate in 1984 and is considered by many to be one of the twentieth century's greatest English poets.

'Wind' is taken from the collection of poems entitled *Hawk in the Rain,* published in 1957. On Channel 4 'The English Programme: Passwords' (1998) Hughes speaks about 'Wind':

> For quite a few years my parents lived in a house on top of a high ridge in West Yorkshire, over the Calder Valley. Either side of this ridge the valleys just dived away out of sight, right down into a gorge and trees and streams…and then on the other side the hillsides rose up very steeply to the moors…

> This is a poem about a gale that went on for a few days and if you've ever been in a gale like that for a while, it gets in your head, begins to affect you.

Glossary

stampeding (l. 3) wild headlong rushing of frightened animals (horses or cattle)

floundering (l. 4) moving awkwardly and with difficulty

astride (l. 4) with one leg on each side

wielded (l. 6) handled a weapon skilfully

brunt (l. 11) probably 'with full strength'

grimace (l. 13) distorted facial expression, such as contempt, pain, disgust

goblet (l. 17) a glass or metal drinking-cup with a stem

entertain (l. 20) consider, think about

What happens?

The poet describes his experience of a raging storm that continues through the night and the next day. The wind is so fierce it dramatically affects the appearance of the landscape and frightens the inhabitants of the isolated moorland house, who can do nothing but 'sit on', feeling vulnerable and recognising the brute force of nature.

Structure

The poem is written in six four-lined stanzas, the regularity in the shape of each contrasting with the wildness of the gale. Do you think that as a poet Hughes recognised it was the only control he could ever have over nature? Each stanza has its **half-rhymes**, holding it loosely together, but there is only one **full rhyme**, on lines 5 and 8. At this point there is a space in time between daybreak and noon, but more noticeable is the change from third person to **first person viewpoint**, where we witness the effects of the storm directly on the narrator.

Line 1 has a steady iambic pentameter metre, but this changes throughout the poem as the storm persists and nothing is secure.

Hughes uses **enjambement** very effectively. Examine how the held pause at the end of line 4 suggests the chaotic din through the long night — 'Till day rose'. Similarly, the overlapping pause at the end of line 16 places emphasis on 'Rang'. 'Or each other' at the start of stanza six comes after a pause between stanzas: the mounting trepidation even denies the comfort of companionship.

Language

Hughes uses black and green to describe the menacing landscape. In the 'darkness' of the night, the winds are 'black' and in the 'blade-light' of day the **colours** become 'luminous black and emerald'. Hughes writes about the setting of 'Wind' in *Poetry in the Making* (1967):

> The grass of the fields there is of a particularly brilliant watered green, and the stone walls of the enclosures that cover the hillsides like a great net thrown over whales, look coal black.

Note also 'the black-back gull' and the 'fine green goblet' all in contrast to the orange dawn sky and the fire in front of which the occupants of the storm-thrashed house huddle.

A selection of violent **action verbs** in the present tense: 'crashing', 'booming', 'stampeding', 'floundering', 'flexing', 'quivering', 'blazing', pull the reader into the drama of the storm.

There is also a clear **timeline** as the poem progresses, so we can share the experience with the speaker. **Language of the senses** describes what can be heard, seen and felt. Stanza one describes the violent noises of the storm **overnight**; stanza two depicts the view of the windswept surreal landscape in the **early morning** light; stanzas three and four describe the personal discomfort of being outside the house at **noon**; line 18 moves into 'Now', the present tense of **late afternoon or evening**. The sensory experience is complete in the final lines when we 'feel' while 'seeing' and 'hearing'.

Hughes uses **alliteration** for particular effects. 'Wind wielded' almost whistles; lines 6 to 8 ('Blade-light, luminous black...') contain many 'l' sounds to create the effect of long, sharp, bright light; the 'f' sounds of 'flap' and 'flung' are sustained before the short vowels sounds to give the impression of being suddenly blown away.

Look at the use of **assonance** in lines 14 to 16, the sharp 'a' sound suggesting the dangerous speed of the wind and its menacing threat to any form of permanence.

Onomatopoeia adds violent sound to the poem: 'crashing', 'booming', 'drummed', 'bang', 'rang', 'shatter'.

Imagery

The dramatic impact of 'Wind' is due to its vivid imagery. The storm is described as though the weather is alive with many uses of **personification**, **metaphor** and **simile**.

- Stanza one **personifies** the wind like a wild animal 'stampeding the fields' or even a monster 'floundering black astride' the landscape. It flashes its sword (l. 7) and visibility is reduced to flashes of 'black and emerald'. On line 13 the fields are 'quivering' and the 'skyline a grimace', attributing pain and distress as far as the eye can see. A magpie appears to be 'flung…away' as it struggles to fly against the force of the gale, the house windows 'tremble' and even the rocks (symbols of strength and stability) 'cry out' in terror.

- The **metaphor** of the first line compares the house to a ship at sea, with its feeling of helplessness as the woods are 'crashing' around like waves and the hills 'boom' with thunder. The speaker 'scaled along the house-side', to get coal, hanging on as though on a steep mountain or ship's mast, his eye-balls 'dented', as though the wind targeted his sight with its painful force. The fixed, unchanging hills seem like flimsy canvas tents and the very foundations of the house feel unstable, as though they could be torn up like tree roots. 'We grip our hearts' concisely describes the terror that reduces mortals to thoughtlessness.

- The three **similes** on lines 8, 16 and 17 describe the wind's effect on three senses. It visibly bends and twists the light 'like the lens of a mad eye', deflects the black-back gull with its unrelenting force 'like an iron bar slowly', and sounds 'like some fine green goblet' about to 'shatter' as its 'note' rises to an insufferable pitch.

> ### Key quotation
>
> The tent of the hills drummed and strained its guyrope,

Ideas to consider

The poet expresses fear in the way the forces of nature transform the countryside and frighten those caught up the storm. He also recognises human helplessness against the elements. Do you think he demonstrates other emotions? Is there any evidence of excitement or admiration?

Types of character and voice

- Which poems explore the alienation of character?
- Which poems explore characters from the past?
- Which poems explore characters in a relationship?

All 15 poems in the 'Character and voice' section of your anthology have been chosen because in some way they deal with this same theme. The characters are explored by the poets, who sometimes write from their own perspective and elsewhere create a persona for their character by writing in the voice of that character. Sometimes the poem's main idea is centred on one particular person; other times we read about individual characters, either real or imagined, named or unnamed, and recognise our own feelings and the ways we behave towards each other.

To help you understand the many ways in which the 'Character and voice' poems can be compared, different aspects of the theme have been put into categories. It is your personal interpretation of the characters presented that is important, so keep an open mind when responding to this theme and make sure you recognise that many poems belong in more than one category.

Alienation

Alienation means the turning away or estrangement from society. The state of being an outsider, of feeling isolated, can mean physical separation, emotional detachment, or often both.

Pause for thought

Can you recognise how Betjeman's father in the poem 'On a portrait of a deaf man' suffered isolation due to his deafness? The walks with his son were 'long' and 'silent' and he sadly could not hear the birdsong. 'He could not hear me speak' the poet writes and we wonder how close the relationship was.

Armitage's 'clown punk' has such an eccentric physical appearance that he seems alienated from others on the 'shonky side of town', where his unsociable habit of pushing his face on to a car windscreen is unlikely to endear him to anybody. It is not known where he lives, whereas two other poems present characters who are definitely homeless: Thomas recalls 'a solitary mister' cruelly treated by schoolchildren in a local Welsh park, and in 'Give' the voice of a desperate homeless person pleads for human understanding and charity.

Medusa begs her unfaithful husband to acknowledge her beautiful and 'fragrant' youth before jealousy fuelled her desire for revenge and alienated her in her 'foul-mouthed' Gorgon state. 'Melia, on the other hand, in 'The ruined maid', wryly accepts social estrangement when choosing prostitution as preferable to the hardship of a moral, yet poverty-stricken, life.

The 'poor, clever girl', Alison, is the unfortunate victim of a head injury that has denied her a fulfilling future and has separated her permanently from her former promising self. The 'horse whisperer' is another victim of events beyond his control when, 'scorned as demon and witch', he is forced to flee, cast out by the arrival of the tractor and farmers growing increasingly suspicious of his skills.

Characters from the past

Some characters are remembered from a poet's own recent past, others are from specific historical times. In 'Checking out me history' Agard protests that the history he has been taught has kept him ignorant of the brave resilient freedom-fighters whose struggles changed the course of Black history, therefore denying him a sense of his own identity.

Ozymandias, an ancient egotistical ruler, desired immortality by building many monuments to symbolise his wealth and power, yet Shelley reflects on powerlessness against the ravages of time and nature. Only the sculptor's 'sneer of cold command' remains. The Duke of Ferrara, another powerful tyrant, is so obsessed with collecting impressive works of art that he fails to appreciate the true living beauty of his young good-natured wife.

Kay describes her childhood reliance on her exciting imaginary friend, 'Brendon Gallacher', and Molloy's past boyfriends provided her with 'the best and worst of times'. Both poets recognise how time has changed: the loss of Brendon when the truth was exposed left the creativity of childhood 'flat out on [her] bedroom floor' and Molloy's new husband, when she was 'wedded, bedded', disregarded all romance and treated her like 'a toy'.

Characters in a relationship

The narrator of 'Singh song!' is delighted with his 'newly bride' and still in the early stages of passion and excitement, neglecting his father's shop by day and staring out at the beaches of the UK late each night, while cuddling up with his nonconformist Punjabi wife. Other characters do not enjoy such happy relationships: jealousy destroys the marriages of Medusa and the Duke of Ferrara. Medusa's marriage was originally full of love for her 'perfect man, Greek God' before 'suspicion' and 'doubt' crept in. The young Duchess of Ferrara 'had a heart...too soon made glad' and was insufficiently impressed by the aristocratic family name to survive a marriage dependent upon power and acclaim.

(Answers to these quick questions are given online)

❶ Which poems name specific historical characters?

❷ In which poems do the poets reflect on their own experiences?

❸ Which poet writes about his father?

Longer questions

❹ Write a paragraph explaining why you feel 'Medusa' by Carol Ann Duffy fits into all three 'Character and voice' categories.

❺ Continue Table 1 so that all 15 'Character and voice' poems are listed down the left-hand side, and tick the appropriate box(es). For some poems you will need to tick more than one box.

Table 1

	Alienation	Characters from the past	Characters in a relationship
The clown punk			
Checking out me history			
Horse whisperer			

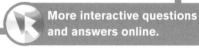

More interactive questions and answers online.

Types of place

- Which poems explore a moment in time and place?
- Which poems explore nature's impact on man?
- Which poems explore man's impact on nature?

The 15 poems in the 'Place' section of your anthology all explore the relationship between human beings and their environment. Some poets use a specific location as the backdrop to their feelings and ideas whereas, for other poets, the setting of the poem is central to their experience. The environments of our daily lives, the locations we visit, the memories of particular places — all such places impact on the way we connect with the earth and consider our place on it.

To help you understand the many ways in which the 'Place' poems can be compared, different aspects of the theme have been put into categories. It is your personal interpretation of poets' purposes and feelings that is important, so keep an open mind when responding to this theme and make sure you recognise that many poems belong in more than one category.

A moment in time and place

Some poets write about their memory of an experience that happened when they were in a particular environment. Jamie remembers one time when, with a group of 'foolhardy' young people, she found herself rowing 'out in the race' of the loch. She undergoes a shifting range of emotions, as do Wordsworth, MacCaig and Hughes in their poems.

Wordsworth's 'act of stealth' with a boat on another lake begins light-heartedly until 'a huge peak, black and huge' causes him to head back in such a frightened state of mind that the spectacle remains to haunt him. As the mountains gather round MacCaig, his initial feelings of intimidation change to gratitude towards 'those marvellous prowlers' and for one moment 'a sunshaft' crowns the mountain, as though sanctifying the scene. In 'Wind' Hughes describes the ferocious power of a moorland storm that terrifies the house's occupants through the night and day and even seems to displace the landscape.

> **Pause for thought**
>
> D. H. Lawrence was visiting the Black Forest area of Germany in July 1929, when he wrote in a notebook: 'Last night a long and lurid thunderstorm poured out endless white electricity…'. Does knowing that a poem is written from a poet's own experience change our appreciation of it?

Nature's impact on man

The impact of water on the human condition is a theme in some of these poems. 'Crossing the loch' and 'Extract from The prelude' both lead to the realisation that a human being is small and insignificant when out in deep water, surrounded by 'hunched hills' and towering mountains. In contrast, however, the experiences offer visual delights in 'the magic dart' of phosphorescence and the 'track of sparkling light'.

Clarke's concerns lie beneath the water. Under the 'troubled surface' of 'Cold Knap Lake' nothing is clear and the water is as cloudy as our memories of childhood incidents. 'The river god' delights in drowning 'fools' who disobey the rules or are 'too bold'. The qualities of 'honest' tap water 'like the straight talk' of the Midlands are celebrated in 'Hard water'. Such 'fierce, lovely water' gave Sprackland an early affinity with the people and places of her youth.

The dramatic pyrotechnics of a thunderstorm amaze Lawrence, who declares humankind has little control over the forces of nature. Brontë's voice is overwhelmed by 'a tyrant spell' that holds her prisoner, coercing her to stay and experience the full force of the developing gale.

Two poets reflect on life and death when they observe birds. Heaney is reminded of the tragic death of his young brother — 'a little stillness dancer' — equating him with the 'nervy goldbeak' blackbird. For Heaney the presence of the bird, sometimes an omen of death, becomes a force for life. Yeats, on the other hand, watches 'The wild swans at Coole' and wonders at their seeming immortality and beauty, while recognising his own advancing age.

Man's impact on nature

'The moment' questions the way human beings grow possessive about land and personal ownership, reminding us that the earth is accommodating us and in our short lifespan we should enjoy our visit, while respecting the power of nature. The exploding 'box of sorrows', however, is no respecter of nature and Clarke describes the suffering of wildlife and humans caught up in the Chernobyl disaster. 'Neighbours' does end in the hope that political openness might prevent future disasters, yet 'London' at the end of the eighteenth century was no place for optimism. Blake's tone of anger and his condemnation of social injustice demonstrate his disgust at the impact of ruling hypocrisy on his home city.

Humankind's attempts to try to command or control nature are futile, as illustrated in 'Ozymandias' and 'Storm in the Black Forest'. There are no competitors against nature's supremacy, just feeble imitation.

Review your learning

(Answers to these quick questions are given online)

1. Which poems have a loch or lake as their setting?
2. Which poems describe bird behaviour?
3. Which poems describe town or city life?

Longer questions

4. Write a paragraph explaining why you think 'Hard water' has been included in the 'Place' cluster.
5. Continue Table 2 so that all 15 'Place' poems are listed down the left-hand side and tick the appropriate box(es). For some poems you will find you need to tick more than one box for the same poem.

Table 2

	A moment in time and place	Nature's impact on man	Man's impact on nature
The blackbird of Glanmore			
A vision			
The moment			

More interactive questions and answers online.

Comparing poems

- **Is it worth doing a plan for my response?**
- **Which aspects of the poem should I compare?**
- **Which are the most important aspects to compare?**

The examination for Unit 2 'Poetry across Time' lasts 1 hour 15 minutes and is divided into two sections. In Section B you have to answer a question on a poem you have not read before (see page 98); Section A requires you to **compare** two poems.

In Section A, you have to choose one question (from a choice of two) from the poetry theme studied, for example, 'Character and voice' *or* 'Place'. One poem is named and you have to **compare** this poem with any other of your choice from the same cluster. The foundation-tier question gives two extra bullet-point reminders in the following format:

Remember to compare
- the characters/places/feelings in the poems
- how these are presented

How do I time-manage my response?

Divide your time as suggested below.

- 5 minutes — write a plan for the named poem and poem of your choice
- 35 minutes — compare the two poems.
- 5 minutes — read through your response to check what you have written and make any last-minute changes.

(Make sure that you do not spend too much time writing about the named poem. The comparison part is equally important.)

If you are entered for the **higher tier** then you should plan your response for the first five minutes, before using the remaining 40 minutes to compare the two poems (one named, the other of your choice).

- Five minutes — write a plan comparing the two poems.
- 40 minutes — compare the two poems.

So how do you make sure that you compare? If you write about two poems without comparing them then you are not going to gain the marks your understanding deserves, even if you show excellent appreciation of each poem.

The Assessment Objective the examiners are looking for wants you to compare and contrast the different ways that poems express meaning and how they do this. Try dividing this objective into four parts for your response.

A four-part plan for your response

1 **What** do I think the poet is saying in poem A?
   How does this **compare** with what the poet is saying in poem B?
2 **Why** does poet A feel like this? Does the poet have a purpose? What is the tone/mood of the poem? Does this change?
   How does this **compare** with poet B's feelings and purpose?
3 **How** does the poet express himself/herself through the techniques used?
   Compare each technique that you write about in poem A with a similar or different technique in poem B. Go to the literature guides website to download tables that will help you to compare poetic techniques.
      (This is an important part of your response, so try to analyse a number of techniques in detail. Select the outstanding techniques used in the poems and compare and contrast them, making sure you analyse their effect on the reader.)
4 **How** do I feel about these two poems?
   Compare your personal response, either expressing a preference and saying why, or explaining the different/similar effect of each poem on your own emotions. See the **Grade focus** below.

'I enjoyed both of these poems, but I prefer 'Brendon Gallacher' to 'The hunchback in the park'. I like the way the boy turns out to be an imaginary friend, because I used to have an imaginary friend, who I treated like a real child. 'Oh, my Brendon Gallacher' suggests she is really sad to give him up, because he was part of her childhood and made life more exciting.'

This answer expresses a preference, explains why, and gives a supporting quotation — grade C.

'Both of these poems gave an insight into their poet's childhood, but I empathise more with Jackie Kay's painful sense of loss, when her imaginary friend, along with her childhood innocence, has to be left behind. 'Oh, my Brendon Gallacher' she cries poignantly at the end. Dylan Thomas remembers the loneliness of the taunted 'solitary mister' of his own childhood and the reader has compassion for the disabled man with his dreams of normality, but Kay's related experience reminds me of my imaginary childhood friend and what it felt like to be six years old.'

This answer explains the preference, gives supporting quotation, then compares the second poem by integrating further appreciation and relevant quotation, before ending with a personal response — grade A.

Grade *focus*

Compare these grade-C and grade-A responses to understand how to make sure that your response finishes in an impressive way.

A quick framework for your plan

Table 3 gives an example of how you could plan your response, using the four-part plan. This is a response to the question:

Compare how poets' attitudes to place are shown in 'Neighbours' and one other poem from 'Place'.

Table 3 Plan for comparing poems

	'Neighbours'	'Spellbound'
What?	Chernobyl 1986 widespread effects	single person 'tyrant spell' desolate landscape
Why?	angry — 'bitter air' sad — 'box of sorrows' hopeful — 'we wait'	fearful unable to escape submits to storm's powers
How? **1**	structure — separate last line three languages caesuras — hope across boundaries	gentle metre regular rhyme — chant? song-like refrain
2	*(Make quick notes on second technique)*	*(Compare/contrast second technique)*
3	*(Make quick notes on third technique)*	*(Compare/contrast third technique)*
How do I feel?	informative 'wing-beats failed over fjords' — emotive	enjoy reading aloud

Using your plan to write and structure your response

Imagine Table 3 is the plan you have quickly devised. Below is just an example of how you could use it for your response. Notice the comparison words in capital letters, which help to make sure you compare.

1 The 'WHAT are the poets saying?' section

Clarke describes the distressing and destructive effects of the 1986 **Chernobyl** nuclear disaster, when poisonous radioactivity was carried vast distances in the wind from the Ukraine and over Scandinavia and Europe. The **effects were widespread**: 'small birds fell', farmers' soil was contaminated and children's health was put at risk. 'Spellbound', **HOWEVER**, only describes the impression of 'wild winds' on **one person**, as a **'tyrant spell'** brings about a sense of mental and physical paralysis. Alone, in a **desolate landscape** as night descends and the storm intensifies, the speaker 'cannot go'.

(Keep this concise, since the next two sections are the most important.)

2 The 'WHY are they saying this?' section

Clarke seems angry that 'a mouthful of bitter air' should bring such misery to people and the environment in many countries. Long after the accident a lamb still 'sips caesium on a Welsh hill' and the rain still holds potential danger for an unsuspecting child. She also recognises the scale of the explosion, calling the nuclear plant 'a box of sorrows', which has released so much fear and disease into the atmosphere, like the opening of Pandora's Box. Towards the end, she moves on to suggest something positive may now be taking place: 'we wait. We watch', she says, for 'one bird returning with green in its voice'. As 'neighbours' countries will hopefully discuss politics and environmental safety more openly in future to prevent another 'Chernobyl'.

The speaker of 'Spellbound' is also **fearful**, but for **DIFFERENT** reasons. Caught up in the drama of a 'fast descending' storm, she is not only **unable to escape** the danger, but even admits that she has **submitted to some supernatural power** and is held in its mysterious spell. 'I will not go', she boldly announces at the end.

(Make sure you have compared the poems before you move on.)

3 HOW? (comparison of techniques section)

The **final line** of 'Neighbours' is **separated** from the other three-lined stanzas. 'Glasnost. Golau glas. A first break of blue' brings together the **Russian, Welsh and English languages** in the hope that countries can recognise their proximity and with fresh political openness prevent a recurrence of such a disaster. The two **caesuras** in the line perhaps make the reader pause to consider how fresh hope could remove physical boundaries when words are so close together. Even countries have no boundaries when the wind blows.

IN CONTRAST to the free verse of 'Neighbours', a **gentle steady metre** runs through 'Spellbound' with its three even stanzas and simple **regular rhyme** scheme, perhaps to give the impression of a mysterious spell or a **chant**. The final line of each stanza has a song-like refrain, but the slight variation in each line shows the change from 'And I cannot, cannot go' through 'and yet…' to 'I will not…'. The decision that she must stay is made as the poem progresses. The vocabulary may be simple but the effect is compelling, like the storm.

(You should carry on now to compare two other techniques, numbered 2 and 3 on the plan — perhaps **imagery** in each poem — or **alliteration** — there are many to choose from, but aim to compare and contrast two or three.)

4 The 'HOW DO I FEEL?' section

I enjoy reading 'Spellbound' aloud, feeling the strong forces of the words pulling me into the developing storm and imagining the 'wastes beyond wastes below', **BUT** 'Neighbours' informs me of the dreadful consequences of a nuclear disaster. 'Wing-beats failed over fjords' is a very emotive description of how the small and innocent suffer and I am very concerned about the dangers of nuclear power programmes.

(Keep this section short.)

Grade *booster*

Make sure you integrate short quotations from both poems throughout all the sections of your response to support your analyses.

(Answers to these quick questions are given online)

1 Which are the two main aspects of the poems that need to be compared?

2 What kinds of word will make sure I compare?

3 How many techniques should I compare?

Longer question

Write a four-part plan for one of the following:

4 Compare how a character's voice is created in 'The river god' and one other poem from 'Character and voice'.

5 Compare how places are shown in 'A vision' and one other poem from 'Place'.

> More interactive questions and answers online.

Writing about an unseen poem

In Unit 2 Section B, both higher-tier and foundation-tier candidates must answer a question on an unseen poem. This involves reading the poem and structuring your answer in 30 minutes. The higher-tier question will have one part; the foundation tier question will be in two parts. Here are examples of the kinds of question(s) you will be asked:

Higher tier

> **What** do you think the poet is saying and **how** does he (or she) present his (or her) ideas?

Foundation tier

> **What** do you think the speaker feels?
> **How** does he (or she) present his (or her) feelings?

Grade *booster*

Practise your response to a poem you have not seen before by using other poems in your anthology. Always write a plan first.

Can you see that both tiers are asking the same question? The plan for your answer needs to contain the same four-part sections that you used to answer Section A of Unit 2. The WHAT? and WHY? sections will help you answer the first part of the question; the HOW? and HOW DO I FEEL? sections will make sure you answer the second part of the question.

Just changing the poet's words into your own words will not get you many marks. You must pick out quotations to explain the poet's purpose and select techniques the poet uses to get his or her ideas across to you. Your personal response is also important.

Tackling the assessments

- **How do I choose which question to answer?**
- **How should I plan my response?**
- **What does PEE mean?**

If your teacher has chosen for you to study Unit 2 'Poetry across time', then you will be answering questions about poetry in an external examination. The poetry questions are worth 35% of your total English literature grade, with 25% for Section A and 10% for Section B, so you need to impress the examiners. It is not only important that you know the poems in your chosen cluster well, it is vital that you know what the examiners are looking for.

Choosing the question

In Section A you will be given a choice of two questions from each themed cluster, so choose carefully. Do not automatically choose the question where a poem you like is the named poem. There is the possibility that you will be able to choose that poem as your own choice in the other question. Instead, look carefully at what the question is asking you to do, before you decide. Open your anthology and look down the list of poems you have studied in your cluster. Then you can easily consider all your other choices, with the details of the question in mind.

Planning your answer in exam conditions

When you have chosen your question, highlight the key words by circling them. Do not worry about marking the anthology — it is your exam and the materials are there for you to mark as you wish.

1 Copy the main part of the question onto the top of your planning page.
2 In freehand draw your three vertical columns and write the titles of the two poems along the top. (See Table 3 on page 96.)
3 Draw four horizontal lines to make your grid, ready to fill in with What?, Why?, How?, How do I feel?.
4 Now make the notes for your plan, keeping an eye on the key words in the question on top. Note how you do not need many words to remind you of your ideas. Shorten titles and just write q for quotation.

Grade *booster*

It is a good idea to make a quick list of comparison words, somewhere on your planning page, to help you to remember to use them.

5 As you write your response, cross off the words in your plan as you transfer the ideas into your writing. This way you will be able to structure your answer and make sure you do not repeat yourself.

Starting to write

The examiners are not expecting you to produce a piece of writing like a formal essay. They are looking to see whether you can meet the Assessment Objectives.

Time is short, so do not waste it on a dull introduction. Attack the question straightaway. Look at the two examples of response openings below. Imagine the question asks:

> Compare the character presented in 'Give' to that in one other poem in the 'Character and voice' cluster.

A I am going to compare 'Give' by Simon Armitage to 'The hunchback in the park' by Dylan Thomas. They are both in the 'Character and voice' cluster but there are similarities and differences.

B The voice of 'Give' is a homeless person, appealing to passers-by for 'change', since he is desperate in his poverty and has nothing left to give. Dylan Thomas presents 'The hunchback' as a character also alienated from society, yet his loneliness would seem to spring from his physical deformity, which sets him apart and makes him a victim of schoolboy 'mockery'.

Notice how A has not yet started to analyse the two poems, whereas B starts immediately to answer the 'What?' section — and already uses relevant quotation. This leaves more time to explore poets' purposes and techniques, the two most important areas.

How do I achieve a good grade?

Using PEE

An important skill you need to practise in order to develop your ideas and achieve a good grade is PEE. The three parts, which your teacher has probably explained to you, are as follows:

- **P**oint —make your point.
- **E**vidence — back it up with words quoted from the poem.
- **E**xplanation — give detail about why this works well.

Grade *focus*

Compare these examples of how to use PEE at grade C and grade A, using Forster's poem 'Horse whisperer'.

Grade C

The horse whisperer can persuade the horses to calm down and do what the farmers want (**Point**). He says 'My secret was a spongy tissue…a charm to draw the tender giants to my hands' (**Evidence**). These words suggest that the horse whisperer knew that the horses would be attracted by scents like rosemary and cinnamon, not that he had special powers (**Explanation**).

Grade A

It is never clear to the reader whether or not the horse whisperer's success with horses is due to detailed knowledge about horse behaviour or special mysterious skills passed down to him (**Point**). He says 'My secret was a spongy tissue…a charm to draw the tender giants to my hands' (**Evidence**). The word 'charm' alone suggests that some kind of magic is being used, yet the scent of rosemary and cinnamon would attract the horses. Perhaps the farmers were not aware of the effect of these herbs and spices in the nineteenth century. Even if the whisperer is using special knowledge, he still has an obvious respect for the 'tender giants' and enjoys working with them (**Explanation**).

It is always a good idea to make sure your **Explanation** is longer and more detailed than the other two parts. Notice how each response answers all **PEE** requirements, but the A grade response has more detail and shows that the candidate develops the idea made in the **Point**.

Achieving a grade C in foundation tier

To achieve a grade C in foundation tier, your answer needs to show the following:
- a thoughtful response to the poet's ideas and techniques (language, structure, form) with quotations and detail to support your opinions
- an appreciation of how the poet's ideas and techniques affect the reader
- a developed and detailed comparison of two poems, in terms of ideas, techniques and their effect on the reader

Achieving a grade A in higher tier

To achieve a grade A in higher tier, your answer needs to show that you can:
- perceptively explore the poems, with close analysis of detail to support your interpretations
- judge the quality of poets' ideas/themes and techniques (language, structure, form), by convincingly explaining their effect on the reader
- compare the ideas and techniques used in two poems by critical analysis

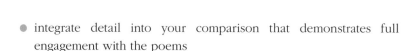

- integrate detail into your comparison that demonstrates full engagement with the poems

Examples of grade-C and grade-A* responses to 'Place' poems

In the extracts below the students are comparing the endings of 'The wild swans at Coole' and 'Crossing the loch'.

Grade-C response

At the end of 'Crossing the loch' Jamie admits that it was 'foolhardy' to take the boat out into the tidal loch. She says they were 'calling our own the sea and salt-water'. But she also remembers the beautiful phosphorescence around their ankles so it must have been a good experience overall. 'The wild swans' has a sadder ending, because Yeats realises that one day he will not be able to watch the swans as he will have died, but the 'mysterious, beautiful' swans will still be there to 'delight men's eyes'.

This answer supports each point with a quotation and a thoughtful explanation, and the same aspect of each poem (the ending) is compared. However, most of this response is interpreting what the poet is saying. It could be improved by:
- exploring the language in more detail
- explaining why the language is effective
- linking these ideas with other words and ideas in the poems

Grade-A* response

At the end of 'Crossing the loch' Jamie admits that it was 'foolhardy' to take the boat out into the tidal loch. 'Calling our own the sea and salt-water' suggests she is fully aware that young people think they can take risks out in the wild and do whatever they choose on the spur of the moment. They seem to think they have control over nature. Experience has taught her that they were lucky to have escaped unharmed with the wonderful memory of 'glimmering anklets' of phosphorescence. In comparison, Yeats' wonderful memory of the swans, when he first saw them 19 years earlier, saddens him immensely, since he realises the effects of the passage of time. He knows 'all's changed'. He must die and envies people who have yet 'to delight their eyes' on these 'mysterious' creatures, symbols to him of eternal love and beauty, whose hearts remain 'unwearied'. The reader suspects the poet has not had success in love in his own life.

This response shows close analysis of detail and clear appreciation of both poets' intentions through the language they use.

Examples of grade-C and grade-A* responses to 'Character and voice' poems

In the extracts below, the students compare the opening stanzas of 'The clown punk' and 'On a portrait of a deaf man'.

Grade-C response

Simon Armitage describes the clown punk in a humorous way in the first stanza. He says he is 'like a basket of washing that got up and walked', so he sounds colourful and scruffy. 'Three times out of ten' suggests that you won't always see him, but he is sometimes there and lives on 'the shonky side of town'. Armitage finishes the stanza with 'But' and goes on to say 'don't laugh' because he doesn't really think it's funny. John Betjeman, on the other hand, is writing about his own father, who has died, so he doesn't poke fun at him. He describes his 'kind old face', his head and his tie and then compares his clothes to 'a closely fitting shroud', which is shocking for the reader.

This answer supports each point with a quotation and a thoughtful explanation. Also the same aspect of each poem (the beginning) is compared and the effect on the reader is considered. The response could be improved by:
- developing the ideas more
- exploring the language in more detail to explain its effectiveness
- analysing the poets' purposes and feelings in their use of language

Grade-A* response

The first stanza of 'The clown punk' seems to depict a humorous character. 'A basket of washing that got up and walked' suggests an untidy heap of clothes. 'Towing a dog on a rope' however, starts to suggest there is something rather sad about this person: often homeless people have dogs as companions. 'But' (followed by the pause between stanzas to create expectation) 'don't laugh' changes the tone. The colourful bundle of clothing isn't funny at all, according to Armitage, who can only foresee this character's future as a shrivelled ink-dyed ageing punk.

Betjeman, on the other hand, is writing about his father, so has no intention of laughing at his father's expense. The first three lines would seem a likely tribute — only someone close to the deceased could recognise that although the tie was bright it was 'discreetly loud'. The final line, however, is shocking: 'a closely fitting shroud' is an uncomfortable image when thinking of a loved one who has recently died, but this sets the pattern for other stanzas, where after description of a live character, sinister, almost grotesque, detail of decomposition is given.

This response shows detailed and developed analysis of language and clear appreciation of both poets' intentions.

Spelling and punctuation

To gain a high grade you need to express yourself clearly and accurately. It is important that your writing is fluent and focused on the question. Make sure you always read through what you have written to ensure your spelling and punctuation are correct.

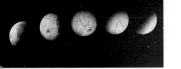

Practice questions

Use the questions below to practise your exam response. Remember to start with a plan.

Foundation tier

1 Compare the ways that poets present character in 'Brendon Gallacher' and one other poem from 'Character and voice'. Remember to compare:
- the characters in the poem
- how the characters are presented

2 Compare your responses to 'The hunchback in the park' and one other poem from 'Character and voice'. Say whether you like or dislike each of these poems and explain why. Remember to compare:
- the characters or ideas in the poems
- how the poems are written

3 Compare how poets show their feelings about nature in 'Spellbound' and one other poem from 'Place'. Remember to compare:
- what the feelings about nature are in the poems
- how the feelings are presented

4 Compare how places are presented in 'Price we pay for the sun' and one other poem from 'Place'. Remember to compare:
- the places in the poems
- how the places are presented

Higher tier

1 Compare how the poets develop a character's voice in 'Les grands seigneurs' and one other poem from 'Character and voice'.

2 Compare how the poets present their characters in 'Casehistory: Alison (head injury)' and one other poem from 'Character and voice'.

3 The relationship between man and nature is explored by some poets in the 'Place' poems. Compare how Wordsworth presents this theme in 'Extract from The Prelude' and one other poem from this cluster.

4 Compare how poets express their feelings about place in 'The moment' and one other poem from 'Place'.

Unit 5: 'Exploring poetry'

If your teacher has chosen for you to respond to poetry as a Controlled Assessment task, then you will have more time to write about and compare the poetry you have studied.

You will be given a question based on poetry linked by one particular aspect: theme and ideas, or genre and form. The poems you choose to compare must be from the English (Welsh or Irish) literary heritage as well as by contemporary poets.

The Assessment Objectives are exactly the same, whether you respond to poetry in an external exam or in controlled conditions in the classroom. The main difference between the two assessment requirements is that you have up to four hours for Unit 5 and are advised to write up to 2,000 words. This means that your response will be more wide-ranging and developed than is possible in a shorter examination.

Sample 'Controlled Assessment' questions

1 Compare the different attitudes to character that can be seen in a range of contemporary and literary heritage poems.

2 Explore and compare the ways poets present their feelings about nature in the contemporary and literary heritage poems you have studied.

3 Which poems from the *Moon on the Tides* anthology do you find particularly memorable? Compare poems from the literary heritage as well as contemporary poems.

4 Imagine you have been commissioned to produce a series of four posters, each with the full text of a poem from 'Place'. Choose two literary heritage poems and two contemporary poems and explain what photographic images you would choose for the border of each poem. Make sure you relate all the images to the language of your chosen poems.

Sample responses

Below are sample extracts from responses to help you to understand how you can demonstrate the required skills. **Remember that for a full response you must compare poets' purposes and ideas as well as poetic techniques and their effects on the reader.**

Character and voice

Writing about poets' purposes and ideas

> 1 Compare how poets present particular characters in 'My last duchess' and one other poem of your choice from 'Character and voice'.

A*-grade response

The Duke of Ferrara narrates the story of his young wife to the Count's envoy and in doing so exposes his own intolerance and jealousy.**1** His ambiguous statement that he 'gave commands; Then all smiles stopped together' suggests a lack of remorse and a conviction that her lack of gratitude for his 'gift of a nine-hundred-years-old name' deserved punishment.**2** Ironically, it is his description of the happy young wife, her heart 'too soon made glad' with delight in courtesy and the simple joys of nature, which contrasts with the arrogant art collector's lack of warmth and dependence on renown and status.**3**

Shelley presents the pharaoh 'Ozymandias' as another tyrannical ruler, this one so obsessed with eternal recognition that palaces and monuments are erected to exclaim his grandeur and omnipotence.**4** 'Look on my works, ye Mighty, and despair', however, becomes a poignantly sad epitaph when all that remains of such a colossus is a 'colossal wreck'.**5** The description of the remaining 'trunkless legs' and 'shatter'd visage' is left to a nameless traveller, the second-hand account highlighting the incidental discovery.**6** The 'wrinkled lip and sneer of cold command' ironically describe the skill of the sculptor and not the 'king of kings': his artistic depiction of a cruel master is all that remains, after the ravages of time and nature.**7** In contrast, the Duchess's portrait with its 'earnest glance', painted by an admiring Frà Pandolf, is still alluring. 'I call that piece a wonder now:' exclaims the Duke, yet the reader recognises the real wonder was the young woman herself who could continue to smile with such an egotistical cold man for a husband.**8**

Margin notes:

1 Insightful response

2 Close analysis of detail to support interpretation

3 Exploratory response to character and its effect on reader

4 Telling detail integrated into comparison

5 Insightful interpretation of effect on reader

6 Evaluation of poet's intention

7 Personal exploratory interpretation

8 Evaluative comparison of ideas

This response shows perceptive understanding when exploring the poets' purposes and the effect of their language on readers. Close analysis of interpretation is supported by detail throughout, quotation is integrated effectively and comparison is evaluative.

Writing about poetic techniques and their effect on the reader

2 Compare how the poets develop character in 'The ruined maid' and one other poem from 'Character and voice'.

A*-grade response

Hardy has written 'The ruined maid' in ballad form: the aabb rhyme pattern and sing-song metre seeming prefect for the satirical tone of the poem.**1** 'One's pretty lively when ruined,' gushes 'Melia, not the response that would be expected from a Victorian farm girl who has resorted to prostitution — or perhaps a 'kept woman' — in order to escape the harsh poverty of the poor. Perhaps Hardy is questioning the hypocrisy of Victorian morality, where wealthy married men could be unfaithful, yet women had to endure poverty whatever the cost.**2** The fourth line of each stanza, like a returning refrain, plays on the word 'ruined' to stress the irony that 'Melia is the well-dressed woman enjoying 'such prosper-ity' and not her previous acquaintance, who she tauntingly reminds is 'a raw country girl'.**3** The first speaker's amazement is conveyed by exclamation marks and the visual splitting of her final word in some stanzas, which together make her seem foolish and naive regarding 'Melia's changed lifestyle.**4**

In comparison, Nagra uses very little punctuation as the speaker recounts the joys of his changed lifestyle now he is married, in this mostly free verse poem.**5** Occasionally full rhymes are used, as in the second and fourth lines of the first stanza. The effect of rhyming '9 o'clock' and 'I do di lock' — is instantly comical as the newly-married man dashes upstairs to be with his wife at every opportunity. The introduction is then 'locked' in place, just as Daljit Nagra makes a clicking sound when he reads his poem, to show Singh's mischievous tone of voice. 'Concrete-cool' and 'stool' also rhyme on lines 45 and 47, to add to the dreamy atmosphere of the 'loved-up' couple 'in di midnight hour'.**6**

The structure of the poem is irregular, in contrast to Hardy's poem: three stanzas begin with the two words — 'my bride' to emphasise his delight in the (rather unconventional) young woman he's so excited to be married to. The question and answer format at the end 'from di stool' expresses the combined delight of the two lovers, in their sentimental sweet-talk. The chorus of shoppers sing out 'Hey Singh, ver you bin?' as they repeatedly taunt the negligent shopkeeper in italic font.**7** This contrast in font styles separates the reality of hard work and public opinion from dreamy young love where 'di brightey moon' turns concrete into 'beaches'.**8**

1 Evaluation of use of form and effect on reader

2 Insightful exploratory response to text and poet's intentions

3 Convincing interpretation of structure, language and poet's purpose

4 Evaluation of effects of punctuation

5 Telling detail integrated into comparison

6 Evaluation of rhyme and its effects on reader; close analysis of detail

7 Evaluation of structure and its effects on reader
8 Insightful exploratory response to presentation

This is an insightful and exploratory response throughout. It evaluates and compares the poets' uses of techniques, selecting a range of telling detail to be integrated into the comparison, while fully exploring the effect on the reader.

Place

Writing about poets' purposes and ideas

> **3** Poems affect readers in different ways and for this reason we dislike some and like others. Write about your responses to 'The blackbird of Glanmore' and one other poem of your choice from 'Place', comparing the poems and explaining why you like or dislike them.

A*-grade response

'The blackbird of Glanmore' is probably my favourite poem in the Place cluster of poems, because it links Heaney's personal tragedy with his thoughts about life and death.**1** These reflections are triggered by the sight of a blackbird 'filling the stillness with life', in complete contrast to the superstition held by a neighbour, around the time of his younger brother's death, that a bird is an omen of death.**2** Throughout the poem, images of the blackbird and his brother seem to correspond: the 'little stillness dancer' is Heaney's description of his brother, dashing to meet him 'so glad to see me home', yet also has echoes of the 'picky, nervy goldbeak'.**3** His father's 'house of death' was in the past and his 'house of life' now has a 'hedge-hop' with its 'stand-offish comeback'. The blackbird only flies a short distance away before returning, always ready to chatter back in its enchanting way. Heaney knows his brother can't physically return but perhaps he also never leaves, often returning as a fond memory. 'It's you, blackbird, I love', Heaney declares, obviously thinking about his 'shortlived' but cheeky, loveable brother.**4**

Norman MacCaig ALSO loves nature and expresses this in 'Below the Green Corrie'. Initially the mountains in the 'dark light' seem 'full of threats', perhaps in the same way that perceiving the appearance of a bird as an omen of impending death would frighten a believer in folklore and superstition.**5** MacCaig soon reverses his mood when he meditates on the powerful effect 'those marvellous prowlers' have had on his life. 'My life was enriched/with an infusion of theirs' is probably the key idea in this poem. The challenges, beauty and dependability of this mountainous Scottish landscape have soaked into MacCaig's consciousness and whatever the weather he is inspired by their presence.**6** The visual image of a 'sunshaft' breaking through the clouds to light up 'that swashbuckling mountain' leaves the poet awestruck with respect for such grandeur and the reader with a wonderful picture of the bold, heroic mountains.

1 Insightful personal response to theme

2 Close analysis of detail to support response

3 Imaginative interpretation of ideas, while evaluating language

4 Convincing further analysis of ideas

5 Evaluative comparison of ideas

6 Exploratory, perceptive response to the poem

The tone of Heaney's 'Blackbird' is also upbeat at the end. The bird is 'in the ivy when I leave' — it hasn't travelled far and like the poet's brother its life may be short. Heaney perhaps reflects that all life is short, but he is 'absolute' for enjoying each brief moment and I agree with this positive viewpoint.**7**

7 Evaluative selection of telling detail integrated into comparison

This response compares two poems by evaluating ideas and themes in an imaginative way. It demonstrates insight into poets' purposes with close analysis of detail, integrating personal response.

Writing about poetic techniques and their effect on the reader

Write about how feelings are presented in 'Wind' and one other poem from 'Place'.

A*-grade response

Ted Hughes and Gillian Clarke both rely on effective imagery to convey their feelings: the first when experiencing a dramatic storm; the latter reflecting on a distant, hazy memory.**1**

1 Telling detail integrated into comparison

In 'Wind' the clamorous gale, which has raged all night, is personified throughout the poem as some vengeful creature, 'stampeding' and destabilising the landscape.**2** From within the isolated house Hughes considers the birds out in the storm: 'The wind threw a magpie away', he writes, comparing the speed of the bird to the disposal of an insignificant piece of litter.**3** In comparison, 'a black-/ Backed gull bent like an iron bar slowly'. Here techniques are combined for visual effect. The gull, its thin, dark elongated shape against the stormy sky, seems to be hovering, riding the force of the gale it flies into. Occasionally, perhaps, its wings slowly dip or lift for navigation as it circles, but the overall effect is one of enjoyment and strength in the face of the storm — definitely in contrast to the fear of the humans below, terrified of the elements.**4** The repetition of the plosive 'b' sound, combined with the single-syllable words, causes the reader to slow down and appreciate the graceful — almost suspended — flight of the gull against the wind and the enjambement between 'black' and 'Backed' insists the reader also pause.**5**

2 Imaginative interpretation of idea
3 Evaluation of poet's use of personification

4 Convincing detailed interpretation of simile

5 Evaluation of other techniques and their effect

Gillian Clarke uses the same techniques between lines 9 and 12. The effect of the alliterative 'drawn by the dread of it' reminds the reader of the voyeuristic tendencies of people near an accident, in this case the possible death of a child. The revived child 'breathed, bleating/and rosy in my mother's hands' and once again the repeated 'b' sound, combined with the enjambement, slows down the reader. There is a sense of relief that the 'bleating' child is alive and the comparison to a newborn delicate lamb perhaps suggests the poet had watched

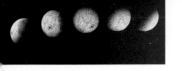

her mother during a difficult lambing. The heroine of the day is certainly the mother who 'gave a stranger's child her breath'.**6**

Whereas 'Wind' describes real experience, the second half of 'Cold Knap Lake' offers different interpretations. Under the 'troubled surface' of the lake there is something 'shadowy under the dipped fingers of willows'. These personified trees are sinister and frightening. Is Clarke suggesting that nature conspired to drown the child, that the trees and swans with their 'heavy webs' are really as frightening as myths and fairytales and not just a beautiful setting for a walk in the park? Clarke's fears seem to be 'under closing water' and linked to how much our memories change and distort with time. She seems to be connecting failing memory with the strange disappearance of 'the poor man's daughter' into the lake.**7**

I prefer 'Wind' with its clear 'luminous' description of a memorable night and day, where the personified elements terrify not only those sheltering from the gale, but even cause the ancient rocks 'to cry out under the horizons'.**8**

This response shows insight when exploring and comparing poetic techniques and their effects on the reader. A range of telling detail is selected, evaluated and integrated into the comparison.